A CHRISTI

A CHRISTIAN LIFE STYLE

A. H. Dammers

HODDER AND STOUGHTON
LONDON SYDNEY AUCKLAND TORONTO

British Library Cataloguing in Publication Data

Dammers, A. H.
  A Christian life style.
  1. Christian life
  I. Title
  248.4   BV4501.2

  ISBN 0 340 38167 1

CONTENTS

INTRODUCTION

In writing this book I have two main objectives. The first is to show that Christians are committed by their faith to work and to pray for 'a more equitable distribution of the Earth's resources and the conservation and development of those resources for our own and future generations', and that this commitment entails a life style of voluntary simplicity, 'living more simply that all of us may simply live'.

My second objective is to commend to my fellow Christians the 'Life Style Movement', which I founded in 1972 as a means whereby those so committed might support each other and promote the growth of such commitment in the world at large. The phrases in quotation marks in the previous paragraph are taken from the Commitment which is undertaken by members of the Life Style Movement.

The first objective occupies my first five chapters. My method is to assemble certain 'testimonies' that are authoritative or authenticating for Christians; the testimonies of the Bible, of Christian tradition, of human reason and of personal experience. Chapter 5 proposes that such a life style of voluntary simplicity is particularly appropriate and indeed urgently necessary 'for today and tomorrow'.

My method for obtaining my second objective is, in Chapter 6, briefly to expound the three seminal documents of the Movement; the Life Style Commitment, the Life Style Guidelines and the Ten Reasons for Choosing a Simpler Life Style. But our Movement does not exist in a vacuum. Since it is concerned with our whole personal style of living, it relates both to our public and to our private preoccupations. Some of these relationships are observed in my final chapter, entitled 'Life Style and . . .'

This book is addressed specifically to Christian believers – and of course enquirers, some of whom may be finding their way to belief through the concerns raised here. But, as is clearly stated in this book, membership of the Life Style Movement is open to women and to men of any religious faith or of none. To be committed to a 'more equitable distribution of the Earth's resources' among the whole human family is an essential part of being fully human.

I should like to thank my daughter Gillian for so professionally preparing the typescript for the publishers.

THE TESTIMONY OF THE BIBLE

The Bible, tradition and reason are all cited as authoritative in various ways for the Christian way of life. All three point us towards a life style which unites us with the whole human family and, indeed, with the whole of God's created universe; which expresses our awareness of the gross injustice with which our Earth's resources are distributed among the members of that human family; and which signifies our solidarity with the poor and with the oppressed. A life style which enables us, in the words of the slogan of the Life Style Movement, to live more simply that all of us may simply live. We shall now look first at the Bible.

THE LAW AND THE FORMER PROPHETS

According to the first of the Creation stories with which the Bible opens, 'the Spirit of God was moving over the face of the waters. And God said, "Let there be light"; and there was light' (Gen. I: 2, 3). The sculptor and writer, Michael Ayrton, has imagined the Creator Spirit, as soon as the light came, perceiving His image on the unruffled surface of the waters below and so being ready with essential assistance when later,

> God said, 'Let us make man in our image, after our likeness; and let them have dominion over the fish of the sea, and over the birds of the air, and over the cattle, and over all the earth,

and over every creeping thing that creeps upon the earth.' So
God created man in his own image, in the image of God he
created him; male and female he created them' (Gen. 1:26,
27).

So, according to the Bible, Homo sapiens is made in the
image of love. Our true nature is expressed in loving God
and in loving one another. Contemporary anthropologists
broadly confirm this latter assertion (e.g. Richard Leakey
and Roger Lewin: *Origins*). The primeval gathering of
nuts, roots and fruit from the 'trees of the garden' (Gen.
2:16; 3:2) was on the whole the co-operative enterprise of
extended families. But as soon as Homo sapiens put his
mind to agriculture – a traumatic experience according to
the book of Genesis (3:17–19) – he felt obliged to own and
to defend his land and his crops from other members of the
species. So he invented war and other violence within the
species, as the story of Cain and Abel demonstrates.

God's question to Cain, the agriculturist, 'Where is
Abel your brother?' is essentially the question which He
puts to us who live in the industrialised North and West of
our planet about our sisters and brothers throughout the
world who are deprived of the necessities of life and so die.
Our response is too often in terms of Cain's reply: 'I do not
know; am I my brother's keeper?' To which God's answer
remains the same today: 'What have you done? The voice
of your brother's blood is crying to me from the ground'
(Gen. 4:9, 10). Nothing in this paragraph, of course, is
intended to deny the central role which agriculture has
played and continues to play in human development. It is
the question of who owns the land that causes the trouble.

According to the collection of ancient and hallowed
stories which form the first part of the book of Genesis it
was Noah whom God chose to save the situation. Noah's
instructions included a concern for and solidarity with the
whole animal kingdom, of which the human family is a
part. To Noah God said,

'I will establish my covenant with you; and you shall come into the ark, you, your sons, your wife and your sons' wives with you. And of every living thing of all flesh, you shall bring two of every sort into the ark, to keep them alive with you; they shall be male and female. Of the birds according to their kinds, and of the animals according to their kinds, of every creeping thing of the ground according to its kind, two of every sort shall come in to you, to keep them alive. Also take with you every sort of food that is eaten, and store it up; and it shall serve as food for you and for them.' Noah did this; he did all that God commanded him (Gen 6:18–22).

The next story (of the Tower of Babel) portrays another major development: that of urban life and of city states whose violent quarrels form the subject-matter of much early history. Language differences remain a major source of division within the human family. With Abraham we enter the shadowy frontiers of history. The Lord called him to a refugee's life style. Abraham retained much of his wealth but had to learn detachment from it. First he had to give up his secure urban life. Second he had to be willing to give up his son and heir, on whom all his hopes rested. Incidentally he generously gave to his companion, Lot, the choice between the fertile Jordan valley and the neighbouring hill country. Abraham is indeed an example to all his spiritual children of that detachment from riches which we so much need today both globally and individually.

But let us move on to Moses, who abandoned his life at court and his status in the household of Pharaoh's daughter for a hazardous life style of solidarity with the oppressed children of Israel. He identified himself completely with them, leaving 'the fleshpots of Egypt' for the harsh, wandering life of the desert. He took upon himself the burdens of leadership and of estrangement from the culture of his youth. Nor did he expect or enjoy the gratitude of those he championed. The story of the exodus is full of 'murmurings' against him. Even his brother and closest collaborator Aaron proved a broken reed in the episode of the golden calf. The first and greatest of the prophets, Moses was also the human agent of God's law. The books of the law that are associated with his name bear a multitudinous testimony to the need for a sharing, loving life style. It was, of course, from them that Jesus plucked out the seminal commandments to love God with all that we are and all that we have and to love our neighbours as ourselves. Written down over the course of many generations, these books spell out compassion even beyond the human family. Thus, 'If you chance to come upon a bird's nest, in any tree or on the ground, with young ones or eggs and the mother sitting upon the young or upon the eggs, you shall not take the mother with the young; you shall let the mother go, but the young you may take to yourself' (Deut. 22:6, 7). Considering the subsistence level at which many of the readers lived, this was a generous and imaginative provision. Particularly in the Book of Deuteronomy, much influenced by the prophetic tradition, there is a great concern for the outsider, the foreigner, the debtor, the poor and the dispossessed. One fascinating example is the provision for debt remission and slave redemption every seventh (sabbath) year and every forty-ninth (jubilee) year (Lev. 25). The whole passage is too long to quote but it has been put forward seriously as a possible principle for dealing with the enormous debts of developing countries today. The institution of the sabbath itself has been, of course, immensely beneficial to the world's poor down the centuries, giving religious sanction to a regular period of release from continuous, exhausting labour.

It is hardly fair to King David to single out for comment from his heroic history Nathan's masterly parable of reproof for David's murder of Uriah and adultery with Bathsheba. But it does provide a near perfect example of the biblical testimony to the necessity of solidarity with the poor.

The Lord sent Nathan to David. He came to him, and said to him, 'There were two men in a certain city, the one rich and the other poor. The rich man had very many flocks and herds; but the poor man had nothing but one little ewe lamb, which he had bought. And he brought it up, and it grew up with him and with his children; it used to eat of his morsel, and drink from his cup, and lie in his bosom, and it was like a daughter to him. Now there came a traveller to the rich man, and he was unwilling to take one of his own flock or herd to prepare for the wayfarer who had come to him, but he took the poor man's lamb, and prepared it for the man who had come to him' (2 Sam. 12:1–4).

David was incoherent with anger against the rich man as his answer shows: '"As the Lord lives, the man who has done this deserves to die; and he shall restore the lamb fourfold, because he did this thing, and because he had no pity." Nathan said to David, "You are the man"' (vv. 5–7). Then Nathan exposed the king's sins in all their horrible details and David immediately expressed his repentance. With what courage and wit had Nathan declared God's word to the wealthy and successful monarch. His parable has a wider, almost universal application. For although we may not commit David's spectacular sins of murder and adultery our Western way of life does collectively take the food out of the mouths of the children of the poor. We pre-empt vast resources of land and water, labour and capital that could otherwise be applied to meeting the basic needs of the very poor.

Elijah's rebuke of King Ahab and his wicked Queen Jezebel for the murder of Naboth so as to acquire his vineyard is in the same tradition of the championship of the poor and the oppressed. Again it is a question of the ownership of land. God's message to Ahab by the mouth of Elijah was direct in all conscience: '"Have you killed and also taken possession? . . . In the place where dogs licked up the blood of Naboth shall dogs lick your own blood"' (1 Kgs. 21:19). Ahab showed signs of repentance and his punishment was deferred. By his boldness Elijah had placed himself in solidarity with the dead Naboth. He took the risk of incurring a similar fate.

THE LATTER PROPHETS

Amos, too, incurred the wrath of the king of Israel and the royal court. A shepherd lad like King David, his gift of prophecy came direct from God. Like Nathan he was a master of irony and suspense. No doubt the people at Bethel cheered his prophecies against their old and new enemies, the Syrians, the Philistines, the Tyrians, the Edomites, the Ammonites and the Moabites. The prophecies against Judah were somewhat nearer the bone, but not objectionable. Finally, however, Amos turns on the people of Israel,

> because they sell the righteous for silver,
> and the needy for a pair of shoes –
> they that trample the head of the poor into the dust of the
>   earth,
> and turn aside the way of the afflicted;
> a man and his father go in to the same maiden,
> so that my holy name is profaned;
> they lay themselves down beside every altar
> upon garments taken in pledge;
> and in the house of their God they drink
> the wine of those who have been fined (Amos 2:6–8).

So the main thrust of their sin is the oppression of the poor. Other prophets take up a similar burden and warn the people that religious observance is no substitute for justice, kindness and humility.

> 'With what shall I come before the Lord, and bow myself before God on high? Shall I come before him with burnt offerings, with calves a year old? Will the Lord be pleased

with thousands of rams, with ten thousands of rivers of oil?
Shall I give my firstborn for my transgression, the fruit of my
body for the sin of my soul?' He has showed you, O man, what
is good; and what does the Lord require of you but to do
justice, and to love kindness, and to walk humbly with your
God? (Mic. 6:6–8).

Hosea (6:6) makes a similar point with commendable
brevity: 'I desire steadfast love and not sacrifice, the
knowledge of God rather than burnt offerings.' According
to St Matthew's Gospel (9:13; 12:7), Jesus twice quoted
the first phrase of this sentence. For English readers of the
Revised Standard Version (which is being used in this
book) it comes out in the more familiar form, 'I desire
mercy and not sacrifice', in the New Testament.

In both the main parts of the book of Isaiah we find
support for our thesis. One of the best-known and most
beautiful passages in the first part of the book (chapters
1–39) gives us an unforgettable picture of the world in
harmony with itself, the realisation of God's kingdom on
earth through the agency of 'a shoot from the stump of
Jesse'.

And the spirit of the Lord shall rest upon him, the spirit of
wisdom and understanding,
the spirit of counsel and might, the spirit of knowledge and
the fear of the Lord.
And his delight shall be in the fear of the Lord.
He shall not judge by what his eyes see, or decide by what his
ears hear;
but with righteousness he shall judge the poor, and decide
with equity for the meek of the earth;
and he shall smite the earth with the rod of his mouth, and
with the breath of his lips he shall slay the wicked.
Righteousness shall be the girdle of his waist, and faithfulness
the girdle of his loins.
The wolf shall dwell with the lamb, and the leopard shall lie
down with the kid,

and the calf and the lion and the fatling together, and a little
   child shall lead them.
The cow and the bear shall feed; their young shall lie down
   together;
and the lion shall eat straw like the ox.
The sucking child shall play over the hole of the asp, and the
   weaned child shall put his hand on the adder's den.
They shall not hurt or destroy in all my holy mountain;
for the earth shall be full of the knowledge of the Lord as the
   waters cover the sea (Isa. 11:1-9).

The combination of righteousness or justice for the poor
and equity for the meek on the one hand and ecological
harmony on the other is just what is required today. So is
the emphasis on the intellectual qualities of wisdom,
understanding and knowledge. For even granting the
corporate will to build a more just and harmonious world,
the intellectual problems are formidable.

In the second part of the book (chapters 40-66) one of
the best known passages concerns the calling of the suffering servant, a calling in which all Christians share. This
representative figure becomes fully identified with the
poor and the oppressed:

He was despised and rejected by men; a man of sorrows and
acquainted with grief; and as one from whom men hide their
faces he was despised, and we esteemed him not. Surely he
has borne our griefs and carried our sorrows; yet we esteemed
him stricken, smitten by God, and afflicted. But he was
wounded for our transgressions, he was bruised for our
iniquities; upon him was the chastisement that made us
whole, and with his stripes we are healed (Isa. 53:3-5).

The suffering servant's identification with the oppressed
is seen to have a redemptive quality. No wonder that
Christians have perceived in this passage a Messianic
prophecy of Jesus Christ.

The testimony of the Wisdom literature however is

more ambiguous, for it contains a substantial witness to the belief that a materially prosperous life style is the reward of well-doing. As a clergyman of the Church of England I have read or heard readings from the Psalms on very many occasions. But I was disconcerted to find that no passage from them immediately sprang to mind in support of my thesis. A reference to the word 'righteousness' in my concordance however soon put me right. Psalm 72, for example, begins with a prayer that the king, who symbolises in his person the rich and powerful, should take up the cause of the oppressed.

> Give the king thy justice, O God, and thy righteousness to the royal son!
> May he judge thy people with righteousness, and thy poor with justice!
> Let the mountains bear prosperity for the people, and the hills, in righteousness!
> May he defend the cause of the poor of the people, give deliverance to the needy, and crush the oppressor! (Ps. 72:1–4).

In Psalm 85 (v. 10), 'righteousness and peace will kiss each other', a happy metaphor for the closeness of the relationship between justice and peace. The future tense in this and other passages indicates hope rather than achievement. The psalmists are conscious of much present injustice. The promise that God 'comes to judge [or rule] the earth. He will judge the world with righteousness, and the peoples with equity [or with his truth]' is twice repeated (Pss. 96:13; 98:9). 'Righteousness and justice' indeed 'are the foundation of his throne' (Ps. 97:2). That is why, 'Blessed are they who observe justice, who do righteousness at all times!' (Ps. 106:3). Such continual righteousness is not merely a question of individual judgments in the courts. It is an attitude, even a life style. In many passages in the prophets righteousness and equity for the poor and the oppressed are set against the correct performance of the cultic acts.

'For I desire steadfast love and not sacrifice, the knowledge of God, rather than burnt offerings' (Hos. 6:6), cries Hosea, twice quoted, according to St Matthew's Gospel, by Jesus (9:13; 12:7). One psalmist at least brings them together in a hymn of the temple, and unites them with the joy which is so essential a feature of an appropriate life style. 'Let thy priests be clothed with righteousness, and let thy saints shout for joy' (Ps. 132:9).

We may conclude this brief section on the Wisdom literature with the observation of Francis Bacon that

> prosperity is the blessing of the Old Testament; adversity the blessing of the New, which carrieth the greater benediction, and the clearer revelation of God's favour. Yet even in the Old Testament, if you listen to David's harp, you shall hear as many hearse-like airs as carols; and the pencil of the Holy Ghost hath laboured more in describing the afflictions of Job than the felicities of Saloman (*Essays*, 5, 'Of Adversity').

Meanwhile Jeremiah had made himself very unpopular with the establishment of his day and had suffered severely for his peace-mongering. He spoke up against God's people's putting their trust in 'chariots and horses', the offensive weapons of his day. The causes of peace and of justice are and always have been intertwined. It is the poor and the oppressed who suffer most from the absence of either.

> Thus says the Lord: 'Let not the wise man glory in his wisdom, let not the mighty man glory in his might, let not the rich man glory in his riches; but let him who glories glory in this, that he understands and knows me, that I am the Lord who practises steadfast love, justice, and righteousness in the earth; for in these things I delight, says the Lord' (Jer. 9:23–4).

Again he proclaims,

> Thus says the Lord: 'Do justice and righteousness, and
> deliver from the hand of the oppressor him who has been
> robbed. And do no wrong or violence to the alien, the
> fatherless, and the widow, nor shed innocent blood in this
> place' (Jer. 22:3).

Ezekiel too carries the same burden, most eloquently in
Chapter 34. There is a sharp contrast between the oppression by the powerful, 'the shepherds', and the compassion
of God.

> Ho, shepherds of Israel who have been feeding yourselves!
> Should not shepherds feed the sheep? You eat the fat, you
> clothe yourselves with the wool, you slaughter the fatlings;
> but you do not feed the sheep. The weak you have not
> strengthened, the sick you have not healed, the crippled you
> have not bound up, the strayed you have not brought back,
> the lost you have not sought, and with force and harshness
> you have ruled them . . . Thus says the Lord God, Behold, I
> am against the shepherds . . . I will rescue my sheep from
> their mouths, that they may not be food for them . . . I myself
> will search for my sheep, and will seek them out . . . I will
> seek the lost, and I will bring back the strayed, and I will bind
> up the crippled, and I will strengthen the weak, and the fat
> and the strong I will watch over; I will feed them in justice
> (vv. 2–4, 10–12, 15, 16).

At a quite different level, a domestic level as it were, the
prophet Daniel testified to the connection between a
simple life style and good health. His motive for refusing
'the king's rich food or . . . the wine which he drank'
(Dan. 1:8) was religious, not altruistic nor medical. He
believed that such food and drink would defile him and his
companions, Shadrach, Meshach and Abednego, so he
asked that they should be 'given vegetables to eat and
water to drink' (v. 12) for a trial period of ten days. At the
end of this trial period 'it was seen that they were better in

appearance' (v. 15) than their contemporaries at court, who had been enjoying the rich food and the wine. So they were allowed to continue in their self-imposed abstinence.

JESUS OF NAZARETH

These powerful strands of solidarity with and compassion for the poor and the oppressed, and of moderation in the acquisition and use of wealth which we find in the Old Testament are the more remarkable by reason of the world-affirming nature of the Jewish faith. Christians believe that these strands unite in the person, the life and the teaching of Jesus Christ. His incarnation itself is the supreme example of solidarity and identification with the poor. God chose that His Son should be born as an Asian villager whose people were subject to an alien imperial power. As St Paul put it to his beloved fellow Christians at Philippi, the fact that the Son of God became man at all is sufficient motive for us to follow in his footsteps.

> Let each of you look not only to his own interests, but also to the interests of others. Have this mind among yourselves, which is yours in Christ Jesus, who, though he was in the form of God, did not count equality with God a thing to be grasped, but emptied himself, taking the form of a servant, being born in the likeness of men. And being found in human form he humbled himself and became obedient unto death, even death on a cross. Therefore God has highly exalted him and bestowed on him the name which is above every name, that at the name of Jesus every knee should bow, in heaven and on earth and under the earth, and every tongue confess that Jesus Christ is Lord, to the glory of God the Father (Phil. 2:4–11).

St Paul shows us that it is on the cross that Jesus reveals God's glory to the uttermost. This is the point at which He is identified most absolutely with the oppressed and the poor.

I remember once during a Bible Study Group meeting in Sheffield studying the account of Our Lord's Passion in St John's Gospel and coming to the word: 'It is finished' (19:30). I made a contribution to the discussion that the Greek word, *tetelestai* has cosmic overtones; that, for John, this word from the cross carried the grand meaning of 'the strife is o'er, the battle won; the salvation of the world is accomplished. Alleluia'. A member of the group whose daily work involved the manipulation of white-hot ingots of steel all day made a different point. 'I've always thought that it meant, "Thank God, that's over", the cry of a man at the end of his tether, exhausted by pain.' Both points are true.

According to John, Jesus's mother, essential agent of the process of incarnation, was present at the Crucifixion. We do not learn a great deal from the Gospels about this Asian village woman, Mary, whom God chose for this blessed task. Her song, the Magnificat, sung daily in countless churches throughout the world, remains an inspiration for all those who would like to detach themselves from the ostentation of riches and identify themselves with the hungry and 'those of low degree'. In the strong light of her own calling, Mary has a vision of the God who

has scattered the proud in the imagination of their hearts,
he has put down the mighty from their thrones,
and exalted those of low degree;
he has filled the hungry with good things,
and the rich he has sent empty away (Luke 1, 51–3).

Many Christians have found in these words a call to political action on behalf of the hungry and the oppressed. Indeed, as we shall see later, such political action is a vital part of any life style of solidarity with the poor.

Other Christians have found a similar political inspiration in Luke's description of Jesus's first sermon; a

description which the evangelist surely intends us to take
as representative of Jesus's preaching:

> And he came to Nazareth, where he had been brought up; and
> he went to the synagogue, as his custom was, on the sabbath
> day. And he stood up to read; and there was given to him the
> book of the prophet Isaiah. He opened the book and found the
> place where it was written,
>
> 'The Spirit of the Lord is upon me, because he has anointed
> me to preach good news to the poor.
> 'He has sent me to proclaim release to the captives and
> recovering of sight to the blind,
> 'to set at liberty those who are oppressed, to proclaim the
> acceptable year of the Lord.'
>
> And he closed the book, and gave it back to the attendant,
> and sat down; and the eyes of all in the synagogue were fixed
> on him. And he began to say to them, 'Today this scripture
> has been fulfilled in your hearing.'
>
> And all spoke well of him, and wondered at the gracious
> words which proceeded out of his mouth (Luke 4:16–22).

This account conveys to us the priorities of the kingdom of
God: 'to preach good news to the poor, to proclaim release
to the captives and recovering of sight to the blind; to set at
liberty those who are oppressed, to proclaim the acceptable year of the Lord.' The story also conveys to us the
urgency of the task, an urgency that remains today, nearly
two thousand years later. 'Today this scripture has been
fulfilled.'

Jesus's own life style is, of course, supported by His
teaching. For many, believers and unbelievers alike, the
high point of all His teaching is found in the Beatitudes,
expressed in two parallel versions, Matthew 5:1–12 and
Luke 6:20–3. These passages set out the life style of the
citizen of the kingdom of God. St Luke's version is simple
and straightforward. The citizen of the kingdom is
poor, hungry, weeping and hated and excluded; in the
modern jargon, marginalised and more than marginalised.

St Matthew's version is more detailed, spiritualised as it were. It is 'the poor in spirit', a precise description of those whose life style is being commended in this book, and not just 'you poor', the original hearers, who are blessed; those who mourn and the meek; those who hunger and thirst, not just literally but 'after righteousness'; again an accurate description of the life style we commend. Such 'hunger and thirst' involves political action, as we shall see, as well as personal moderation. 'The merciful' also are blessed. The English word 'mercy', though beautiful enough, doesn't quite encompass the fullness of the Hebrew concept on which the New Testament Greek relies. As we saw in referring to Hosea 6:6 it carries the meaning of 'steadfast love' as well as the more juridical associations of the English word 'mercy'. Compassion comes into it, a word which by derivation implies solidarity. So here, too, is a precise pointer to the life style we envisage. Purity of heart, expressed in a transparency of love for the whole human family, comes next. Peacemakers are those who positively work for peace rather than just hope that it will come along. Finally persecution and unpopularity as a result of a passion for more justice in the world, 'for righteousness' sake', are a sure mark of the truly Christian life style. Until I came to write this paragraph I hadn't realised how precisely and in detail the Matthaean version of the Beatitudes describes the life style that this book is concerned to promote.

If, as has been suggested, for many people the Beatitudes represent the high point of Jesus's teaching, for others this high point is found in His parables, particularly the best-known stories such as those of the Good Samaritan, the Prodigal Son, the Rich Man and Lazarus, the Labourers in the Vineyard. A high proportion of these marvellous stories are in fact 'parables of sharing' in which one of the lessons taught is that the sharing of resources is a powerful sign of God's kingdom. Thus the Good Samaritan shares with the wounded man his ass, his wine and oil, his money, his time and energy. Indeed he risks his life for him, for it is an old trick for robbers to set up a decoy to trap the unwary. He shares everything with the poor and oppressed traveller before him. Another point that we gain from the story is that the marginalised and despised Samaritan is as good and as real a person as anyone else; an essential lesson to be learned if we are to be true members of the human family.

Similarly in the parable of the Prodigal Son, the father shares everything with his sons. He gives his younger son the share of property that falls to him (Luke 15:12). To his older son he says, 'all that is mine is yours' (Luke 15:31). Above all he shared with them his love. 'But while he [the younger son] was yet at a distance, his father saw him and had compassion, and ran and embraced him and kissed him' (Luke 15:20). To his elder son, even when the latter was at his most ungracious, he said: 'Son, you are always with me' (Luke 15:31). By contrast this elder son stands condemned in the story as a non-sharer, grudging even the holding of a party to celebrate his brother's return.

The story of the Rich Man and Lazarus, which follows in the next chapter (Luke 16:19–31), is also about sharing and non-sharing and their eternal significance. By worldly standards the rich man was a decent enough fellow. He even spared a kind thought for his five brothers while he himself was in the anguish of hell. But his life style was totally unconcerned with the beggar at his gate. The whole world lies at our gate today and Moses and the prophets, to say nothing of Jesus Himself, exhort us to do what we can about the injustice of it all. In Bristol Cathedral, where I work, we have a contemporary painting of Lazarus at the rich man's gate by Peter Koenig. He carries a lily, a symbol presumably of that purity of heart which attains the heavenly vision. The dog which is affectionately licking his sores is female and black. The other dog which is snarling aggressively at him is male and white. The rich man's house is a country mansion, such as rich men still inhabit, at the end of a drive. Its door, which ought to be open and a sign of welcome, is totally obscured by a large lock on the gate. So the picture draws out some of the symbolism from the story. The rich man's fatal failure lies in his remoteness and unconcern.

All these three parables of the kingdom occur in St Luke's Gospel. Of course St Luke is recognised as being personally sympathetic to the poor, to women and to other oppressed groups. But he is not the only evangelist who discovers such a sympathy in the Jesus whom they portray. The parable of the Labourers in the Vineyard is found in St Matthew's Gospel (20:1–16) and demands some examination. In this story the rich man, the local landowner, is portrayed as a just and caring person. He gets up early and goes personally to the village square to hire the day labourers. He doesn't leave this to his steward, for he himself knows the village men. He chooses a good team, sufficient for the work, and returns home. But he can't get out of his mind the disappointment of those who fail to get work, whose families therefore probably will not eat that day. So he goes back at intervals throughout the day to see if any men are persisting in their desire for work. Each time he has compassion on these unemployed, the true meaning of the Greek word *argous*, translated 'idle' in the Revised Standard Version. At the end of the day he makes a point of having the last-comers paid first. To each he gives the same wage, a subsistence wage no doubt, sufficient for their daily bread. The first-comers naturally thought that they would get more. To them he paid what was due. For God's justice, Jesus teaches us, is different from most men's. He is generous and merciful to those in greatest need, but without being unjust to the others. Probably the early Christians applied this story to the great issue of the salvation of the Gentiles. 'So the last will be first and the first last' (Matt. 20:16). But it is also capable of a more earthy, a more direct, application, the distribution of work opportunities thoughout the global village.

St Matthew's Gospel (25:31–46) also contains the story of the Last Judgment or the Great Assize. This is not so much a parable as a word picture in story form which summarises so much of the teaching which has been under review in this chapter. All the nations, that is, the whole human family, are judged eternally according to whether they have given food to the hungry, drink to the thirsty, clothes to the naked, and according to whether they have visited those who have been ill or in prison. The King in the story is identified with the 'Son of Man', that is, Jesus Himself, and proceeds to identify himself with the hungry and thirsty, the naked and the prisoner. So must his followers.

Gospel stories about Jesus are as illustrative as his parables of his identification with the poor, the oppressed and the marginalised. One further illustration may here suffice. In the fourth Gospel (John 4:3ff.) we find a detailed account of Jesus's meeting with a Samaritan woman at the well. The story's basic meaning is as a textbook example of personal evangelism. As so often in this Gospel the story carries secondary meanings, one of which concerns how Jesus affirms the dignity of the oppressed. Then as now the shortage of immediately available clean water is the effective sign of poverty. It is always the women who have daily to carry every drop of precious water from its source to their homes. For most village women in Asia and Africa there is at least the consolation that this daily toil 'gets them out of the house', provides them with an opportunity of social life with their peers, and enables the unmarried to be seen and admired. This consolation, however, was denied to the woman whom Jesus met. She was marginalised by reason of her notoriety, her sex and her 'race', and her membership of a despised 'ethnic minority', the Samaritans. Yet Jesus chose her as His first missionary to her people, His first apostle to them. As St Paul became the apostle to the Gentiles without being a member of the Twelve, so she became the apostle to the Samaritans. (A point to be considered when the authority of Scripture is called in as an aid to delay the ordination of women in the Church of England!) There is some (indirect) evidence that her apostolate was successful. (cf. Acts 8:4ff.)

'. . . he [Jesus] left Judea and departed again for Galilee. He had to pass through Samaria' (John 4:3–4). In fact He did not have to pass through Samaria. Jews travelling from Jerusalem to Galilee often went the long way round via Decapolis in order to avoid the danger of contamination by the hated Samaritans. But He did have to pass through Samaria in the profound sense that there were people there who needed Him. As He said later, His food was 'to do the will of him who sent me, and to accomplish his work' (v. 34).

'So he came to a city of Samaria, called Sychar, near the field that Jacob gave to his son Joseph. Jacob's well was there, and so Jesus, wearied as he was with his journey, sat down beside the well. It was about the sixth hour' (vv. 5–6). I have visited that well, one of the most ancient and most authentic of all the biblical sites. You can't move a well!

'There came a woman of Samaria to draw water. Jesus said to her, "Give me a drink." For his disciples had gone away into the city to buy food' (vv. 7–8). She came at midday to avoid the gossip of the other women of the village. Jesus put Himself in her debt by asking her for a drink. That is a good way to uphold the dignity of the marginalised and oppressed. It was not, however, a technique to secure that end. He was genuinely thirsty. Her reaction was predictably negative, emphasising all that separated her from Him. 'The Samaritan woman said to him, "How is it that you, a Jew, ask a drink of me, a woman of Samaria?" For Jews have no dealings with Samaritans' (v. 9). Nor in most cultures do strange men address themselves to unaccompanied women. Jesus now begins to 'evangelise' in terms of her everyday concerns and His. In Britain the natural first topic of conversation is often the weather. In a majority of the world's villages it would be the state of the local water supply. Fortunate, indeed, is the village that has living, that is, running water in its well.

'Jesus answered her, "If you knew the gift of God, and who it is that is saying to you, 'Give me a drink,' you would have asked him, and he would have given you living water"' (v. 10).

She is intrigued with this strange man, not yet persuaded but already speaking of what unites them ('our father Jacob') rather than, as previously, of what divides them. 'The woman said to him, "Sir, you have nothing to draw with, and the well is deep; where do you get that living water? Are you greater than our father Jacob, who gave us the well, and drank from it himself, and his sons, and his cattle?"' (vv. 11–12). Is her tone wholly ironic or has the possibility entered her mind that here, indeed, is one who is 'greater than our father Jacob'?

'Jesus said to her, "Every one who drinks of this water will thirst again, but whoever drinks of the water that I shall give him will never thirst; the water that I shall give him will become in him a spring of water welling up to eternal life." The woman said to him, "Sir, give me this water, that I may not thirst, nor come here to draw"' (vv. 13–15). Jesus has brought her to the point at which, without fully understanding what is happening, she wants what He has to offer – the essential first step in evangelism. Now that He has won her confidence, He is in a position to challenge her.

'Jesus said to her, "Go, call your husband, and come here." The woman answered him, "I have no husband." Jesus said to her, "You are right in saying, 'I have no husband'; for you have had five husbands, and he whom you now have is not your husband; this you said

truly"' (vv. 16–18). From the fact that she had come
to draw water at midday and, we may assume, from her
general demeanour, Jesus could have guessed as much.
But the evangelist represents Him as deadly accurate in
his knowledge. She reacts, as might have been predicted,
by changing the subject, moving on to the safer ground of
theological controversy. 'The woman said to him, "Sir, I
perceive that you are a prophet. Our fathers worshipped
on this mountain; and you say that in Jerusalem is the
place where men ought to worship"' (vv. 19–20).

At this point many of us would have been tempted to
humiliate her by pointing out how she was evading the
issue; but not Jesus. He safeguards her dignity by taking
her question seriously. Indeed His answer provides a basis
even now for our relationship with those of other faiths.
'Jesus said to her, "Woman, believe me, the hour is
coming when neither on this mountain nor in Jerusalem
will you worship the Father. You worship what you do not
know; we worship what we know, for salvation is from the
Jews. But the hour is coming, and now is, when the true
worshippers will worship the Father in spirit and truth,
for such the Father seeks to worship him. God is spirit,
and those who worship him must worship in spirit and
truth"' (vv. 21–4). When this Gospel was written it is
most probable that both Jerusalem and Samaria had been
destroyed by the Romans. The point is that Jesus both
makes exclusive claims for the Jews and inclusive claims
for all who worship the universal Father 'in spirit and
truth'.

'The woman said to him, "I know that Messiah is
coming (he who is called Christ); when he comes, he will
show us all things." Jesus said to her, "I who speak to you
am he"' (vv. 25–6).

So He has made such an impression on her that the
Messiah comes into her mind. She associates the Messiah
with 'the hour' to which He had referred. The time is now
ripe for Him to tell her the good news. 'I . . . am he.' This

is the essence of the Gospel, the most primitive Christian creed. 'Jesus is Lord.' The timing is superb. 'Just then his disciples came' (v. 27). They were surprised to find Him talking with a woman, but made no comment.

'So the woman left her water jar, and went away into the city, and said to the people, "Come, see a man who told me all that I ever did. Can this be the Christ?" They went out of the city and were coming to him' (vv. 28–30). The woman is not named in the story, for she represents us all. All Christians, though unworthy as she was, are called to be evangelists. When she becomes aware who Jesus is she forgets everything else in her excitement, even her water pot.

Many Samaritans from that city believed in him because of the woman's testimony. 'He told me all that I ever did.' So when the Samaritans came to him, they asked him to stay with them; and he stayed there two days. And many more believed because of his word. They said to the woman, 'It is no longer because of your words that we believe, for we have heard for ourselves, and we know that this is indeed the Saviour of the world' (vv. 39–42). Their experience of the Gospel becomes personal. But nothing can take from the despised and marginalised woman whom Jesus met at the well, the honour due to her as the first apostle to her people.

THE EPISTLES

Reference has already been made to St Paul's letter to his fellow Christians at Philippi. That letter ends with an acknowledgment of their generosity.

'And you Philippians yourselves know that in the beginning of the gospel, when I left Macedonia, no church entered into partnership with me in giving and receiving except you only; for even in Thessalonica you sent me help once and again. Not that I seek the gift; but I seek the fruit which increases to your credit. I have received full payment and more; I am filled, having received from Epaphroditus the gifts you sent, a fragrant offering, a sacrifice acceptable and pleasing to God. And my God will supply every need of yours according to his riches in glory in Christ Jesus. To our God and Father be glory for ever and ever. Amen' (Phil. 4:15-20).

Their generosity of spirit was matched by his. As he writes, he was

circumcised on the eighth day, of the people of Israel, of the tribe of Benjamin, a Hebrew born of Hebrews; as to the law a Pharisee, as to zeal a persecutor of the church, as to righteousness under the law blameless. But whatever gain I had, I counted as loss for the sake of Christ. Indeed I count everything as loss because of the surpassing worth of knowing Christ Jesus my Lord. For his sake I have suffered the loss of all things, and count them as refuse, in order that I may gain Christ and be found in him, not having a righteousness of my own, based on law, but that which is through faith in Christ. (Phil. 3:5-9).

So Paul gave up everything that had been most precious to him – his status as a Hebrew and a Pharisee, obedient to the law of God – to gain solidarity in Christ with His beloved Gentile converts, the previous outsiders, ethnically, morally and culturally.

The Philippian Christians had been generous to Paul and he was duly grateful. Even closer to his heart, however, than his own needs was the collection for the Jerusalem church which he pressed on his Gentile converts as a sign of their faith. In this insistence on 'partnership with me in giving and receiving' (Phil. 4:15) he is at one with the general feeling of the New Testament letter-writers.

Thus in I John we read: 'But if any one has the world's goods and sees his brother in need, yet closes his heart against him, how does God's love abide in him? Little children, let us not love in word or speech but in deed and in truth' (3:17–18). James, who in some sense stands at the opposite theological pole to Paul, has this to say about attitudes to the rich and to the poor.

> For if a man with gold rings and in fine clothing comes into your assembly, and a poor man in shabby clothing also comes in, and you pay attention to the one who wears the fine clothing and say, 'Have a seat here, please', while you say to the poor man, 'Stand there', or 'Sit at my feet', have you not made distinctions among yourselves, and become judges with evil thoughts? Listen, my beloved brethren. Has not God chosen those who are poor in the world to be rich in faith and heirs of the kingdom which he has promised to those who love him? But you have dishonoured the poor man. Is it not the rich who oppress you, is it not they who drag you into court? (Jas. 2:2–6).

One of the clearest testimonies to the dangers of wealth and the need to be moderate in our life style is found in the pastoral epistles (I Tim. 6:6–10), a passage which forms a fitting climax to this brief selection from the 'testimony of the Bible' to the need for a life style of solidarity with the poor and detachment from riches. Live more simply that all of us may simply live.

> There is great gain in godliness with contentment; for we brought nothing into the world, and we cannot take anything out of the world; but if we have food and clothing, with these we shall be content. But those who desire to be rich fall into temptation, into a snare, into many senseless and hurtful desires that plunge men into ruin and destruction. For the love of money is the root of all evils; it is through this craving that some have wandered away from the faith and pierced their hearts with many pangs.

2

THE TESTIMONY OF CHRISTIAN TRADITION

The testimony of Christian tradition as a whole may be distinguished but not separated from the testimony of the Bible. The Bible indeed enshrines the first and definitive stage of the tradition. From the beginning the life style of the Church was a sharing life style, as we read in the Acts of the Apostles (4:32–5):

> Now the company of those who believed were of one heart and soul, and no one said that any of the things which he possessed was his own, but they had everything in common. And with great power the apostles gave their testimony to the resurrection of the Lord Jesus, and great grace was upon them all. There was not a needy person among them, for as many as were possessors of lands or houses sold them, and brought the proceeds of what was sold and laid it at the apostles' feet; and distribution was made to each as any had need.

This extraordinarily other-worldly behaviour was no doubt in part the result of a widespread belief that the end of the world was imminent anyway. But it has provided a practical inspiration for many initiatives of sharing ever since, both inside and outside the Church. To become a Christian in the early centuries generally meant to identify yourself with the poor and the oppressed. There were 'not many wise according to worldly standards, not many powerful, not many of noble birth' (I Cor. 1:26) among the first converts. From the beginning persecution was always a possibility and often a reality.

ST BASIL, ST AUGUSTINE, ST BENEDICT

Moreover, no sooner did persecution by the state fade away than monasticism arose to replace it as the model of Christian discipline and witness. Of detachment from worldly goods St Basil the Great (AD 330–79) wrote as follows:

> The rich take what belongs to everyone, and claim they have the right to own it, to monopolise it . . . What keeps you from giving now? Isn't the poor man there? Aren't your own warehouses full? Isn't the reward promised? The command is clear: the hungry man is dying now, the naked man is freezing now, the man in debt is beaten now – and you want to wait until tomorrow? 'I am not doing any harm,' you say! 'I just want to keep what I own, that is all' . . . you are like someone who sits down in a theatre and keeps everyone else away, saying that what is there for everyone's use is his own . . . If everyone took only what he needed and gave the rest to those in need, there would be no such thing as rich or poor. After all, didn't you come into life naked; and won't you return naked to the earth? . . . The bread in your cupboard belongs to the hungry man; the coat hanging unused in your closet belongs to the man who needs it; the shoes rotting in your closet belong to the man who has no shoes; the money which you put in the bank belongs to the poor. You do wrong to everyone you could help, but fail to help.

That is severe indeed. But there is no reason to believe that St Basil, one of the great founding fathers of corporate monasticism, did not practise what he preached. St Augustine of Hippo (AD 354–430) is traditionally associated with a Rule which, in both its masculine and its feminine forms as we have received them, is rooted in the biblical passage from Acts quoted above. It begins as follows:

1 The Basic Ideal: Mutual love expressed in the Community of Goods and in Humility.

1 We urge you who form a religious community to put the following precepts into practice.

2 Before all else, 'live together in harmony' (Ps. 133:1), 'being of one mind and one heart' (Acts 4:32) on the way to God. For is it not precisely for this reason that you have come to live together?

3 Among you there can be no question of personal property. Rather take care that you share everything in common. Your superior should see to it that each person is provided with food and clothing. He does not have to give exactly the same to everyone, for you are not all equally strong, but each person should be given what he personally needs. For this is what you read in the Acts of the Apostles: 'Everything they owned was held in common, and each one received whatever he had need of' (Acts 4:32, 35).

Lest it be said that St Basil and St Augustine were writing only for 'heroic' Christians, the heirs of the martyrs, it should be added that they were also inheriting a tradition of universal sharing. Thus in the Didache, or Teaching of the Lord through Twelve Apostles, to the Gentiles, a compendium of instructions for a Christian way of life from the second century AD, we read: 'Share everything with your brother. Do not say, "It is private property." If you share what is everlasting, you should be that much more willing to share things which do not last.' It was the genius of St Benedict to draw these various strands together, providing a humane yet detailed Rule for his brothers which weaned the monastic life from the competitive extremities of asceticism. The Rule's prologue ends with the words:

But if anything be somewhat strictly laid down, according to the dictates of sound reason, for the amendment of vices or the preservation of charity, do not therefore fly in dismay from the way of salvation, whose beginning cannot but be strait and difficult. But as we go forward in our life and in faith, we shall with hearts enlarged and unspeakable sweetness of love run in the way of God's commandments; so that never departing from His guidance, but persevering in His teaching in the monastery until death, we may by patience share in the sufferings of Christ, that we may deserve to be partakers of His kingdom. Amen.

Private property was as rigidly excluded by St Benedict as by St Augustine.

The vice of private ownership is above all to be cut off from the Monastery by the roots. Let none presume to give or receive anything without leave of the Abbot, nor to keep anything as their own, either book or writing-tablet or pen, or anything whatsoever . . . Let all things be common to all, as it is written: 'Neither did anyone say that aught which he possessed was his own.' But if any one shall be found to indulge in this most baneful vice, and after one or two admonitions do not amend, let him be subjected to correction (Rule, ch. 33).

Again the influence of Acts 4:32–5 is clearly seen. However, there is no prescription for a soulless egalitarianism, but rather for a pastoral concern for individual needs, as the next chapter (34) 'Whether all ought alike to receive what is needful' makes clear:

As it is written: 'Distribution was made to every man, according as he had need.' Herein we do not say that there should be respecting of persons – God forbid – but consideration for infirmities. Let him, therefore, that hath need of less give thanks to God, and not be grieved; and let him who requireth more be humbled for his infirmity, and not made proud by the kindness shown to him: and so all the members of the family shall be at peace. Above all, let not the evil of murmuring shew itself by the slightest word or sign on any account whatsoever. If anyone be found guilty herein, let him be subjected to severe punishment.

Both St Augustine and St Benedict were concerned with the practical difficulties that arose from the widely differing social and economic backgrounds of their members. A life style that would seem exceedingly simple, even harsh to one, would feel secure and comfortable to another. Each member has to be treated as the individual he or she is.

Presumably these problems have long since largely disappeared in Western monasticism, but they continue to loom large in any attempt to construct a distinctively Christian life style in the world today. Considerable indignation was aroused when a writer in our *Life Style Movement Quarterly Newsletter* suggested that no member ought to run a car. I have myself often gone on record with the opinion that no one in a small country like Britain needs a private motor car of more than 1300cc or possibly 1500cc. Even this I would qualify, in allowing some kind of minibus to a family with a large number of dependent children. What is the truth about such a matter? Are people's real needs widely differing? Of one thing I am certain: no one in this country needs a large, fast private motor car. Should they therefore be abolished? In his last chapter (73, 'That the whole observance of Perfection is not set down in this Rule') he humbly tells us:

We have written this Rule, in order that, by observing it in Monasteries, we may shew ourselves to have some degree of goodness of life, and a beginning of holiness. But for him who would hasten to the perfection of religion, there are the teachings of the holy Fathers, the following whereof bringeth a man to the height of perfection. For what page or what word is there in the divinely inspired books of the Old and New Testaments, that is not a most unerring rule for human life? Or what book of the holy Catholic Fathers doth not loudly proclaim how we may by a straight course reach our Creator? Moreover, the Conferences of the Fathers, their Institutes and their Lives, and the rule of our holy Father Basil – what are these but the instruments whereby well-living and

obedient monks attain to virtue? But to us who are slothful
and negligent and of evil lives, they are cause for shame and
confusion. Whoever, therefore, thou art that hasteneth to thy
heavenly country, fulfil by the help of Christ this least of
Rules which we have written for beginners; and then at length
thou shalt arrive, under God's protection, at the lofty sum-
mits of doctrine and virtue of which we have spoken above.

The intention behind the Life Style Movement and the
Life Style Commitment is precisely similar. This least of
Commitments is 'written for beginners' as a light along
their path.

ST FRANCIS

Down the centuries, however, even St Benedict's humane
way of life became corrupted. There arose, therefore, a
series of reforms in the direction of austerity; Cluniac,
Cistercian and so on. Meanwhile another great star arose
in the firmament, St Francis, bridegroom of the Lady
Poverty. There is an early portrait of Francis at Subiaco,
St Benedict's first retreat. We know it to be early as it bears
no halo. But he and his Friars Minor struck out on a
distinctive path. It has even been said that there are two
basic approaches to a truly Christian life style; the moderate, ordered way of St Benedict and the disruptive, passionate, heroic way of St Francis. However that may be,
the latter certainly demands our attention.

St Francis appears both to have preached and practised
not so much detachment from worldly goods as their
rejection; not so much the sharing of them as their total
giving away. Yet he remains a pattern and an inspiration
for those who would live more simply, that all of us may
simply live by reason of the total solidarity with the poor
and the oppressed which he attained. The best-known
example is probably that decisive embrace of the leper.
But the story which I find as good as any to characterise this

extraordinary man is the story of his discourse on perfect
joy to Father Leo (ch 8, *Little Flowers of St Francis*).

One winter's day, as St Francis was going from Perugia with
Friar Leo to St Mary of the Angels, suffering sorely from the
bitter cold, he called Friar Leo, that was going before him,
and spake thus, 'Friar Leo, albeit the Friars Minor in every
land give good examples of holiness and edification, neverthe-
less write and note down diligently that perfect joy is not to be
found therein.' And St Francis went his way a little farther,
and called him a second time, saying, 'O Friar Leo, even
though the Friar Minor gave sight to the blind, made the
crooked straight, cast out devils, made the deaf to hear, the
lame to walk, and restored speech to the dumb, and, what is a
yet greater thing, raised to life those who have lain four days in
the grave; write – perfect joy is not found there.' And he
journeyed on a little while, and cried aloud, 'O Friar Leo, if
the Friar Minor knew all tongues and all the sciences and all
the Scriptures, so that he could foretell and reveal not only
future things, but even the secrets of the conscience and the
soul; write, perfect joy is not there.' Yet a little farther went St
Francis, and cried again aloud, 'O Friar Leo, little sheep of
God, even though the Friar Minor spake with the tongues of
angels and knew the courses of the stars and the virtues
of herbs, and were the hidden treasures of the earth revealed
to him, and he knew the qualities of birds, and of fishes, and
of all animals and of man, and of trees, and stones, and roots,
and waters; write – not there is perfect joy.' And St Francis
went on again a little space, and cried aloud, 'O Friar Leo,
although the Friar Minor were skilled to preach so well that he
should convert all the infidels to the faith of Christ; write – not
there is perfect joy.' And when this fashion of talk had
endured two good miles, Friar Leo asked him in great wonder
and said, 'Father, prithee in God's name tell me where is
perfect joy to be found?' And St Francis answered him thus,
'When we are come to St Mary of the Angels, wet through
with rain, frozen with cold, and foul with mire and tormented
with hunger; and when we knock at the door, the doorkeeper
cometh in a rage and saith, "Who are ye?" And we say, "We
are two of your friars," and he answers, "Ye tell not true; ye

are rather two knaves that go deceiving the world and stealing the alms of the poor; begone!" And he openeth not to us, and maketh us stay outside hungry and cold all night in the rain and snow; then if we endure patiently such cruelty, such abuse, and such insolent dismissal without complaint or murmuring, and believe humbly and charitably that that doorkeeper truly knows us, and that God maketh him to rail against us; O Friar Leo, write – there is perfect joy. And if we persevere in our knocking, and he issues forth and angrily drives us away, abusing us and smiting us on the cheek, saying, "Go hence, ye vile thieves, get ye gone to the spital, for here ye shall neither eat nor lodge"; if this we suffer patiently with love and gladness; write, O Friar Leo – this is perfect joy. And if, constrained by hunger and by cold, we knock once more and pray with many tears that he open to us for the love of God and let us but come inside, and he more insolently than ever crieth, "These be impudent rogues, I will pay them out as they deserve"; and issues forth with a big knotted stick and seizes us by our cowls and flings us on the ground and rolls us in the snow, bruising every bone in our bodies with that heavy stick – if we, thinking on the agony of the blessed Christ, endure all these things patiently and joyously for love of Him; write, O Friar Leo, that here and in this perfect joy is found.'

As so often in profound matters, so here it is by means of a story that we come most effectively at the truth. This story illustrates St Francis's complete solidarity with the poor and the oppressed. On the whole it does not fall to the oppressed, or, for that matter, to any but a tiny minority to give sight to the blind, restore speech to the dumb, or know all tongues, sciences and Scriptures, or the courses of the stars and the virtues of herbs or to be brilliantly successful evangelists. But it is open to the oppressed, indeed it is their daily diet, to be excluded and beaten. St Francis's solidarity with the oppressed is firmly rooted in his consuming passion for solidarity with Jesus Christ in his oppression. As he further explains to his friend, Friar Leo:

And now, Friar Leo, hear the conclusion. Above all the grace and the gifts of the Holy Spirit that Christ giveth to His beloved is that of overcoming self, and for love of Him willingly to bear pain and buffetings and revilings and discomfort; for in none other of God's gifts, save these, may we glory, seeing they are not ours, but of God. Wherefore the Apostle saith, 'What hast thou that is not of God, and if thou hast received it of Him, wherefore dost thou glory as if thou hadst it of thyself?' But in the cross of tribulation and of affliction we may glory, because this is ours. Therefore the Apostle saith, 'I will not glory save in the cross of our Lord Jesus Christ.'

Meanwhile, in the Eastern Church the spirit and practice of St Basil was maintained and developed and is with us today. One brief example must suffice at this point, a quotation from the Ecumenical Press Service Report (December 7th, 1978) of a consultation on the 'Orthodox approach to Diakonia':

Christian diakonia today requires a revival of the spirit of asceticism, i.e. of self-denial and of concern for our neighbour, leading to a more simple life style . . . For this reason diakonia includes the necessity to liberate man from whatever oppresses, enslaves and distorts the image of God, in order to open the way for redemption. In this sense diakonia (service) is a liberation for salvation.

POST-REFORMATION – ILLUSTRATIONS FROM ENGLAND

The Reformation also includes within the wide sweep of its reforms a rebellion against the venality, extravagance and wealth of the Church and a radical return to biblical insights, not least those of the Old Testament prophets. In England, if I may for a few paragraphs of this brief survey of Christian tradition confine myself to my native land, both the main traditions of reformed churchmanship reflected a certain moderation of life style which is authentically Christian. The word 'Puritan' today carries a mainly negative image. But in such a person as John Milton the Puritan way of life encompassed both a discreet and moderate style and a splendour of imagination and sensitivity. The other main tradition, that of the Established Church, is best characterised by such a parish priest as George Herbert, who abandoned the prospects of a brilliant worldly career for the modest life style of a devoted country parson and Christian poet. In the eighteenth century John Wesley proved himself to some extent an heir to both traditions. His life style appears to have been as moderate as it was strenuous. His solidarity with the spiritual aspirations of the Kingswood miners distinguished his ministry at an early stage and estranged him from his bishop, the scholarly Joseph Butler. The Methodism that arose out of his ministry and that of his followers is named for the disciplined life style of its adherents. A passionate concern both for those who were deprived, for reasons of geography or history, of the knowledge of Christ and for those who were oppressed by the triumphs of the industrial revolution remained a hallmark of the evangelical revival which followed the Wesleys' preaching.

Nonconformist Christians, including Quakers, were largely responsible for the abolition of the slave trade on the one hand and for the Factory Acts on the other, both major protests against the greed with which the market economy was operated. Leaders of the Oxford Movement also expressed their active concern for the poor and the oppressed both at home and overseas. A high proportion of the most devoted 'slum parsons' were Anglo-Catholics, and the selfless work of Anglican sisters in the cholera and other epidemics is not forgotten. These traditions of solidarity with the oppressed continue to operate within both the Anglo-Catholic and the Evangelical traditions in the Church of England and are strong also within the Free Churches and in the Roman Catholic Church in this country. Indeed they are a feature of the Ecumenical Movement in Britain as in the world as a whole. The World Council of Churches has from the beginning taken very seriously its responsibilities in setting a style of solidarity with the poor. Its Project to Combat Racism has been among the best-known examples, if only because of the opposition it has aroused. In Britain Christian Aid remains a department of the British Council of Churches, but dwarfs its parent in terms of resources. Roman Catholics, too, in many parts of the world have been to the fore. In South America and elsewhere they have taken the lead not only in the development of liberation theology but also in the political action that flows from it. Here, for example, is a song from Latin America which, at a popular level, firmly roots such theology in the doctrine of the Incarnation:

> Since He came into the world and into history;
> Broke down silence and suffering;
> Filled the world with His glory;
> Was the light in the coldness of our night;
> Was born in a dark manger;
> In His life showed love and light;
> Broke hardened hearts
> But lifted up dejected souls;
> So today we have hope;
> Today we persevere in our struggle;
> Today we face our future with confidence,
> In this land which is ours.
> (Quoted in 'A Common Account of Hope'. Faith and Order
>   Commission, World Council of Churches.)

Largely owing to modern mass communications which bring into our homes the global issues of justice and peace, there must be today a greater total awareness of the need for solidarity with the poor by the Church than ever before. This general awareness, however, has not yet penetrated on the whole to the logical consequences for our personal life style. Even the awareness is patchy and ambiguous. Consider for example the General Synod of the Church of England. At the time of writing this body has been rather good at inviting others to redress injustice and repudiate oppression. Excellent debates have issued in impeccable resolutions on, for example, the British Government's Nationality Bill, apartheid in South Africa, transnational companies, the Brandt reports, unemployment and so on. The debate on 'The Church and the Bomb' produced a resolution which called on the Government to repudiate any first use of nuclear weapons. But when it is the Church of England itself which has to show love and concern for 'outsiders', its record has been almost wholly negative. At the time of writing the Synod has rejected Anglican-Methodist reunion, the covenant, the ordination of women to the priesthood and the licensing of women lawfully ordained overseas for example. Hope on these latter issues, however, is by no means dead.

To sum up: even so hasty a run through Church history as this may suffice to show that Christian tradition is generally at one with the biblical witness in seeking a life style which unites us with the whole human family, and particularly with the poor and the oppressed; and which protests against the gross injustice with which our world is organised; a life style which demonstrates a bias to the poor by living more simply that all of us may simply live.

3

THE TESTIMONY OF REASON

So far so good; but the testimony of reason is more difficult to establish. Reasonable men and women can differ radically not only on secondary issues but even on fundamental ones. It is with confidence, however, that I shall put forward first two general propositions and then particular ones relating to the four elements of a Christian life style which I wish to distinguish; the elements of prayer, prophecy, political action and personal moderation. I shall use the formula 'It stands to reason', and see whether I can carry the reader with me.

IT STANDS TO REASON

First, then, it stands to reason that if the Bible and Christian tradition in general both support the adoption of a life style which by means of its moderation expresses solidarity with the poor, and which does not claim for itself an inordinate share of the earth's resources, then those Christians who are not compelled to such a life style by their own poverty, should voluntarily adopt it.

I hope that I have already written enough in the first two chapters to enable that 'if' to be changed into 'since', or 'because'.

Second, it stands to reason that if, as Gandhi has put it, there is enough in the world for everyone's need but not enough for everyone's greed, then the greedy ought to consume less, to enable the needs of the needy to be met. How about this 'if'? Well, it is demonstrable that there is not enough for everyone's greed since at present up to a thousand million people live in extreme deprivation. Moreover, the overwhelming evidence is that there is in fact enough cultivable land, enough water, enough mineral and other resources, enough labour and capital to sustain a population much larger than the present one. Once more, reason validates both the premiss and the conclusion.

There is also a valid logic of prayer as an essential element of the appropriate Christian life style for today and tomorrow. For it stands to reason that, if God is love and loves all His children, then he wants us all to be liberated from all forms of oppression, including the oppression of extreme deprivation. If that is what He wants, then He is pleased when we pray for such liberation and is inclined to answer our prayers.

Here the premisses that God is love and loves His children cannot be proved. They are however basic axioms of the Christian faith.

It also stands to reason that when we pray for such liberation, when, for example, we pray in Jesus's own words and according to His command, 'Give us this day our daily bread', we commit ourselves to doing what we can to enable our fellow members of the human family to obtain their daily bread.

Here there is no premiss to require verification, only the establishment of a logical link between prayer and action.

There is also an essential logical link between prophecy, that is, the declaring of God's will and God's word as we perceive them, and a Christian life style for today and tomorrow. For it stands to reason that any such movement as Life Style, which, as I have already made clear, embraces members of any faith or of none, has to be missionary. In general this is so for all movements whose members believe that they have an idea whose time has come, an idea which is in fact true. For truth in general has to be communicated. But in particular this is so for Life Style because until it is massively successful, it has little or no impact on the world of political power and economic reality.

So it stands to reason that members of the Life Style Movement are called to be prophets, sharing what they believe, both in word and in deed.

POLITICS AND ECONOMICS

So we come naturally to the logic of political action. This is to prophecy as deeds are to words. Political action is a major instrument of change, the way of getting things done. It stands to reason, therefore, that those who long for a more just and peaceful world should be politically active. We can discern three main levels of political action – international, national and local. We should be active in championship of the poor and the oppressed, whether in opposition to tyranny and violence at home and abroad, or in improving the terms of trade for poor nations, or in increasing the percentage of our own gross national product allotted to development aid, or in conservation or anti-pollution policies. The good causes are legion which demand our thoughtful and constructive support. Even more important, however, is the search for a radically new political direction. For it does seem to stand to reason that market capitalism in general favours the rich and the powerful, as also does the State socialism of Eastern Europe. We need a new economic analysis for our times, comparable in its breadth and depth to that delivered by Karl Marx a century ago.

In days of old when knights were bold, political and economic power was concentrated in the hands of the land-owning class, with the king at the apex of the feudal

pyramid. In the wake of the Renaissance and the Reformation, the rising merchant and capitalist class challenged
the feudal powers. It was by withholding their capital that
they destroyed the divine right of kings, a process which
culminated in England in the execution of King Charles I
in the course of a civil war. The capitalists and merchants
generally retained their political and economic power until
in the late nineteenth century the workers in turn learned
the trick of combining to achieve power by withholding
their contribution, that is, their labour.

The power conflict between capital and labour continues to rage in many countries. But it is also in process of
being replaced by a new combination at the expense of the
consumer. Capitalists increasingly find it convenient to
accede to the demands of the workers and pass on the
consequent price increases to the unfortunate consumers.
An obvious consequence of this continual raising of prices
by those who have the power to do so, that is the producers
of goods and services, is inflation. The consumers, of
course, include the increasing number of the economically
powerless – pensioners, children, the unemployed, a
majority of women.

Each transfer of power, from land-owners to capitalists,
from capitalists to workers, has of course only been
partial. The incumbents have never given up their power
without a fight. It is important to understand that each
transfer has been largely achieved by the next aspirants in
line combining to withhold their essential contribution.
The capitalists refused to lend money to the king. The
workers combined to strike or at least threaten to strike.
Now it is the turn of the consumers world-wide. 'Consumers of the world unite. You have nothing to lose but
your enslavement to unjust and unsatisfying patterns of
consumption!'

But how can the consumers, who include so many
powerless people – the old and the children, a majority of
women, the unemployed, the poor and the hungry –

combine to compel the producers, capitalists and workers together, to give priority to the real needs of the human family – food, clothing, housing, basic health and education services and so on? History suggests first that most, if not all, revolutions begin with the bourgeoisie and second that the way to obtain economic power is to withhold, or at least threaten to withhold, your essential contribution to the economic process. At the end of the day the consumers hold the trump cards. As Adam Smith, prophet of market capitalism, observed: 'The consumer is king.'

To realise this power, those of us who are rich enough to have a measure of purchasing power have to combine to withhold this from the purchase of goods and services which we neither need nor want. This would sooner or later force the producers to stop producing such goods and services and to concentrate their energies on socially useful products. Let me illustrate the point by two examples. I have already mentioned large, fast cars. If we stop buying them, the producers will no longer make them. Consider also tobacco products. In both of these examples what I am proposing is already happening to some extent. But as in the previous transfers of power, from land-owner to capitalist, from capitalist to worker, we shall need a massive, well-disciplined political movement to achieve our aims. There is, however, a distinct possibility that this, the final major transfer of economic power (for are not all the members of the human family basic consumers?) could be achieved without the customary violence. For can we imagine people being FORCED to buy cigarettes or Jaguar cars or any of the thousand and one absurd adjuncts to our consumerist society? Here is a political and economic movement in which Christians can and should join with a clear conscience and on behalf of the thousand million members of our human family who have little or no purchasing power. I wish that I had the skill and the learning to write a whole book on this one point. It could be the most important point that I have to make.

PERSONAL MODERATION

The fourth element in a Christian life style for today and tomorrow is personal moderation. Here again it stands to reason that if we are to be sincere in our prayers for a more equitable sharing of the Earth's resources and in our prophecies of God's word to a feverishly consumerist society and in our political actions and attitudes then we must practise what we preach by adopting a life style of personal moderation. The logical connection is surely self-evident and brings to a close a series of such self-evident propositions, which I believe to constitute a sufficient testimony of reason to the contemporary need for us to adopt a deliberately simple life style. It is with this fourth element, personal moderation, that the Life Style Movement has been most clearly concerned; though I hope that we have not been neglectful of the other three elements to which I have referred: that concentration on our personal source of inspiration which for Christians is prayer; that proclamation of truth in and out of season which for Christians is prophecy; and that concern for 'getting things done' which bears fruit in political action.

4

A PERSONAL TESTIMONY

By the order in which I have presented these testimonies in which the three traditional sources of authority, the Bible, the tradition and reason precede this personal testimony I have intended to demonstrate that it is the former three on which my case rests. Yet it is not inappropriate to append the latter when dealing with so personal a matter as our own life styles. The experiences which have led me to take the stance which is described in this book and to found the Life Style Movement must be relevant to the issue before us.

AT SCHOOL

First has to come what may appear a somewhat naïve understanding of the power and place of prayer in an appropriate life style for today and tomorrow. When I was about 10 years old and away from home at boarding-school, I seemed to myself and others happy enough. Maybe there was more stress in our lives than we realised. Work and games were highly competitive. We were separated from our parents for eight months in the year. There was some, though not much, bullying and some fear of the headmaster's cane. At any rate a number of us, including myself, acquired the unpleasant habit of biting our nails. Some parents offered their sons bicycles or other major bribes if they would desist from the habit. My parents would never think of such a thing. So, as a last resort, I fell to prayer about it -- the first time I had ever really prayed about anything – adding each night to my conventional prayers an explicit request that the habit be removed from me. After about a week, it was never to return except briefly after I had been wounded in the Second World War. There was nothing remarkable about this, nothing contrary to reason. But the experience implanted in me a lasting conviction that simple petitionary prayer is a worthwhile activity. 'If you then, who are evil, know how to give good gifts to your children, how much more will your Father who is in heaven give good things to those who ask him!' (Matt. 7:11).

It was at my next school that the next relevant experience arose. During well over a decade of attendance at various boarding-schools I must have heard hundreds of sermons. But I must confess that I remember none of them. What I do remember, however, are a few of the preachers who particularly impressed me by their integrity. A Christian convert from Sikhism in a light blue turban was one. A rector, whose name escapes me, from the Isle of Dogs was another. He paced up and down in the sanctuary of our school chapel, I remember, showing us the small size of the homes of some of his parishioners. Sir Reginald Kennedy Cox, a small bird-like man in a double-breasted blue suit, was another. He was warden of our College Mission, Dockland Settlements in Canning Town, later to become the Mayflower Centre. We nicknamed him Sir Reginald Kennedy Cadger, but we respected his enthusiasm for his life's work. Then there was Brother Douglas, joint founder of the Society of St Francis, who impressed me the most of all. On reflection I can see that what united all these men in their very varied ministries was their commitment to the poor and the oppressed not only in word but in their way of life. The Indian had identified himself thoroughly with the poor pilgrims of all faiths in his country. The rector from the

Isle of Dogs had chosen to live in what, between the wars, was a sadly depressed area. So had Sir Reginald. Brother Douglas, of course, shared the life of the many 'gentlemen of the road' at a time of high unemployment and patchy welfare provisions.

AT WAR

The Second World War began when I was still at school. It was as a junior officer in the Royal Artillery in the Western desert in 1942 that I came to experience something of the impact of the 'mystery of the incarnation' on the world at large and for me personally. At El Alamein we took part with our twenty-five pounders in the tremendous opening barrage. We formed part of the Tenth Armoured Division and the next morning engaged with our fire, at long range, some counter-attacking enemy tanks. There was great excitement, and indeed a ragged cheer went up, when we were told that we had scored a direct hit and disabled a tank. This was quite a professional achievement at our first effort and seemed to set a seal on all our comradeship and mutual effort up to that time.

A few days later we moved forward and happened to occupy the very scene of our first triumph. The disabled tank was still there, the badly burned bodies of its crew remaining in the attitudes in which they died as they tried to escape. The smell and the flies were awful. We could see and smell the consequences of our excellent teamwork. Excellent it was. Our motives on the whole were good: patriotism, love of our families and friends, defence against a monstrous tyranny. We were uncomplicated in our perceptions and generous in our attitudes. Yet the result was this: the stinking, charred bodies of young men like ourselves. It was at this point that there came to me the personal conviction that only the God whose love is stronger than death and who, at the same time, identifies

Himself thoroughly with our predicament of suffering and sin can save us from that sin. We ourselves, even at the point of our greatest human glory, our finest achievements, are the poor in spirit and the oppressed by sin with whom God identifies in the incarnation of His Only Beloved Son.

LEARNING THE JOB

So it was to offer for ordination training and to read theology at Cambridge that I came home, nearly two years later, after being wounded in the battle for Monte Cassino. This study of theology is the next experience that I wish to offer. I can still recall the beginning of the first lecture I attended on the Old Testament. The lecturer, Dr Henry Hart, began by asking us whether we knew in what book the following words appeared: 'Shall not the Judge of all the earth do right?' We did not. So he pointed out that they might well have occurred in any of the books but were in fact found in the Book of Genesis (18:25). This was a neat way of drawing our attention from the start to the overriding theme of God's righteousness, His justice in the world. This great theme shone through the technicalities of detailed biblical studies, shone through the lives also of at least some of our teachers. My own theological supervisor, Canon Wilfred Knox, for example, was a man of great simplicity and generosity of life style. Of the two other men who (as I recall) took Part II (New Testament) of the theological tripos in my year, one, Geoffrey Paul, worked for many years in the Church of South India. He was, in fact, my predecessor at St John's College, Palayamkottai. The other became Brother Barnabas, of the Society of St Francis. Both, therefore, adopted life styles which variously identified them with the poor.

There is a sense in which the first chapter of this book is a belated tribute to that teaching some forty years ago. On the completion of my formal training for ordination, like many of my contemporaries, I attended to the call to 'Go North, young man'. So my wife and I took up residence in Adlington, near Chorley, on the edge of the Lancashire coalfield, where I served my title as assistant curate. I have not forgotten my first house visit there. I was so green that I called at tea-time. Charlie and his wife welcomed me in warmly. 'Get thi legs under t'table, lad,' he said. This little parable of sharing made me immediately feel at home. Soon afterwards I attended my first death-bed. Mrs Pilkington was the elderly widow of a miner who had died of a pulmonary infection many years before. She lived alone in a tiny cottage near the church. When I arrived her daughter was standing crying at the foot of the bed. Mrs P had not spoken or moved for several hours. I put my face near to hers and said a prayer. Suddenly she stirred, raised herself up, flung her arms round me and kissed me. Then she fell back exhausted. She died that afternoon. Here was another parable of sharing. This poor, old, dying lady gave to me, a stranger, the most precious thing in all the world: her love.

My second curacy was very different, in the wealthiest parish in Birmingham, the Old Church at Edgbaston. The work included responsibility for the daughter church of St Monica's and some lecturing on the New Testament and tutoring at Queen's College, the theological college that was in the Parish. Teaching New Testament studies confirmed me in my conviction that Jesus and his disciples were thoroughly identified with the poor and the oppressed. It confirmed me also in my desire to serve and to learn more in a developing country. Therefore, after just over two years, we went from there to the Church of South India.

INDIA

Memories crowd in at this point – of lessons learned from our Indian friends and acquaintances, of parables of sharing. As chaplain and lecturer in English at St John's College, Palayamkottai, in the diocese of Tirunelveli I was shielded from much direct contact with the harshest realities of extreme poverty, yet I found plenty to admire in the courage and the cheerfulness of the poor.

I remember once spending a few days with some Christian students from our own and other colleges among the Christian tribespeople at Anakkarai. Indian missionaries had encouraged these people to come out of the forests, where they had lived in tree houses, to cultivate the land, learn Tamil and become Christians. Each settlement was surrounded by a bank and ditch as a protection against wild elephants. I remember visiting the hut of a woman whose husband had been trampled to death by such an elephant. She had next to nothing. Yet she entertained us hospitably and her faith was radiant. It was as a learner that I sought to identify myself with her attitudes and situation.

The students at St John's formed an 'Evangelistic Band' which used to visit the surrounding villages. I would accompany them sometimes in the very junior role of children's entertainer. I would take a football, usually the first time such a thing had been seen in the village, and organise an impromptu match, then show the children pictures of Jesus's parables (the Rich Fool was a favourite) and explain them in halting Tamil. Meanwhile, the students would visit the homes and invite the people to a magic-lantern show as dusk fell. One student would then speak or preach. I remember asking one shy 18-year-old whose turn it was for the first time what he was going to say. 'I shall give my testimony; what else can I do?' he replied. (An answer which may dimly have conditioned the form of the first four chapters of this book, some thirty years late.)

Then there was the occasion when we were miles from home in our Ford Popular, driving along a rough road near the seashore. Our fan belt broke and, as this was the first time, we had no spare. But a fishing village was near. One of the fishermen had been in the army during the war and knew what to do. He expertly spliced a rope to replace the broken belt and sent us on our way, adamantly refusing any reward or payment. Another parable of sharing.

One of our best friends is Joseph Vedasiromani, at that time principal of St John's College, also professor of politics and economics. He stood as godfather to our younger son who, like our younger daughter, was born in India. I once remarked on how few books he had in his house, and he replied: 'I don't need to own books. When I've read a book I usually give it to a student who can't afford to buy it.' I myself own hundreds of books and gain comfort from their presence. If I were ever to sell them and give the money for the oppressed it would be because of the example of my friend. Incidentally, before leaving for India I called on a neighbouring vicar friend, Mr Leathem, then of St John's, Harborne. He was a scholar whose tools were books, but he said, 'I'd like you to choose any book in my library as a present.' Here is another parable of sharing, an example of that detachment from worldly goods which we have to cultivate.

One day at Palayamkottai a young man called at our house and asked for some food. He bore himself with dignity and had strong hands. The well in his village had dried up and he had walked some thirty miles and was now near his destination, the town of Tirunelveli, where he would look for work. I asked my cook to prepare some rice and curry for him and sat with him on the veranda as he ate it. I greatly admired his initiative and determination. I think that it was on that occasion that I first fully grasped the intimate connection between praying, 'Give us this day our daily bread', and doing something about it. My new friend, who was not a Christian, was 'doing something about it', for himself and his family. And so ought I, regularly and systematically.

The link between prayer and action is demonstrated also in the story of another friend whom I shall call Jacob. A story which, like some of the others in this section, I have already told in my book *Great Venture*, published by Highway Press in 1958, but long since out of print.

I first heard about Jacob after Evensong one Sunday. I understood that he was a well-to-do Christian who was correspondent or chairman of governors of a local church school. He thought that he and the school were being discriminated against by local authority officials on the grounds of their religion. There was apparently little or no substance in this allegation, but Jacob decided to fast as a protest. When I first heard of him I was told that he had already been fasting for about three weeks down by the river Tambrapani which flows between Palayamkottai and Tirunelveli. I decided that I should like to take the Holy Communion to Jacob the next morning. I thought that this effective sign of God's love for us in Christ might help him to break his fast. I told my colleague at the church, Dr Kantayya, who was both an honorary presbyter and a practising medical doctor, and he offered to come with me.

The next morning at dawn, the best time in the Indian day, I got on my bike, called my friend and together we cycled the few miles down to the river. Jacob was there, lying on his mat near the bridge. I asked him if he would like to receive the Holy Communion with us and his eyes lit up with pleasure. While I prepared the bread and wine, Dr Kantayya took his pulse and asked him about his health. Then the three of us shared the sacrament in the quiet of the early morning.

It would have been good to have been able to report that

the sacrament had a healing effect on Jacob's obstinacy. But it was not so. Nor did anything that I or the bishop or anyone else could say. Eventually, however, when he was very weak, Jacob allowed a friend of his to bring a jutka (a kind of horse-drawn taxi) and take him home with him. This act of kindness broke through all barriers and Jacob expressed himself willing to eat. Dr Kantayya was called and advised on diet. The last time that I saw Jacob he was rational and calm, about to go on a short holiday in neighbouring Sri Lanka.

I have told this story because it tells of the only occasion that I have knowingly administered the Holy Communion to a starving man. For me it illustrates the connection between the common meal which is one thing that the Holy Communion is and the fulfilment of the basic material needs of the poor and hungry. I am convinced that the fourth Evangelist was historically correct in his linkage of the Eucharist with his account of the miraculous feeding of the multitude. I believe that there is evidence in the other three (synoptic) Gospels also that Jesus intended to use that occasion as a great acted parable of His death and new life and that the compassionate physical feeding of the multitude played a significant part in His ministry.

SHEFFIELD

After four years in India we returned home to Britain where I became a parish priest in Sheffield. One day the BBC came to Holy Trinity, Millhouses. We felt rather pleased with ourselves to be chosen as the venue for an act of worship which was to go out on the World Service. Our complacency was somewhat punctured, however, when we learned that it was because we were near Doncaster, where the outside broadcasting equipment had been required at the races the day before. Anyhow we took the opportunity very seriously. Our choirmaster rehearsed the choir to the top of their ability. I wrote and rewrote my sermon. The congregation turned up in force, the ladies wearing their hats and best clothes as if it had been television.

All went according to plan until, as I got into the pulpit to give the final blessing, the producer thrust a grubby bit of paper into my hand carrying the legend: 'We're well within time; add an extra prayer.' I blurted out the first prayer that came into my head, the well-known prayer of St Richard of Chichester: 'O most holy Jesu, most merciful redeemer, friend and brother; may we love you more dearly, know you more clearly and follow you more nearly; for your own dear sake. Amen.'

Some days afterwards I received a letter from a lady who lived in Jerusalem. She wrote that she had lost her faith some forty years previously when her only and much-loved brother had been killed in the closing stages of the First World War. Her heart had been filled with a long-standing bitterness. But she had switched on the radio on coming into her flat that day and had heard the words 'Most holy Jesu, most merciful redeemer, friend and *brother*', and had realised in a flash that He was truly her brother, closer to her than the brother she had lost so many years ago. Her faith had returned in a flood of joy and she wanted us to know.

So I learned, at a deeper level than before, that the Holy Spirit often likes to work through the unconsidered trifle. Out of all our carefully rehearsed and prepared offerings He selected this unrehearsed addition for His great purpose. So it is often through the poor and those without apparent resources that He works most mightily.

At Millhouses we became the first parish in the diocese to mount one of those, at that time, new-fangled stewardship campaigns. Being a suburban parish we believed that we had the skills to do without the help of a professional fund-raising company. Diocesan stewardship advisers were unknown at the time. One churchwarden was a bank manager, the other a businessman, and the campaign secretary a retired income tax inspector who certainly knew what he was about! Our financial aims were to double our income and treble our giving away. Both were achieved and I for one hoped that the latter achievement would help us all to realise, not only by what Mgr Ronald Knox used to call 'the acid test of the collection plate', our interdependence and solidarity with those poorer than ourselves.

COVENTRY CATHEDRAL

The next step, or stop, after eight happy years in Sheffield, was Coventry Cathedral where I became a canon residentiary, director of studies and education officer. One of my many concerns was with what came to be called the Common Discipline, a written commitment which was undertaken first by members of the cathedral staff, then after a few years by members of the congregation and finally, after a few years more by members of other Christian communities throughout the world which were linked with us in what became known as the Community of the Cross of Nails.

Shortly after I joined the staff of Coventry Cathedral the provost suggested that I should spend a week at the great Benedictine abbey at Ottobeuren in Bavaria. I had never been to Germany and spoke only a few words of the language. 'What would you like me to do there?' I asked. 'You don't have to do anything. Just go and live there and see whether you discover something there that I discovered – or perhaps something else.' Ottobeuren already had close links with Coventry. For example, at the world première of Benjamin Britten's *War Requiem* in Coventry Cathedral, Hans Sellschop, who was present, had a vision of a great performance in Germany. This was in due course realised with the composer as conductor, Dietrich

Fischer-Dieskau and Peter Pears as the German and English soldiers, and the Coventry Cathedral choristers. There was a Coventry Cross of Nails on the central altar in Ottobeuren Abbey.

In a Paper read to the first international conference of the Community of the Cross of Nails at Ottobeuren in 1972 I described how that experience led to the formation of a Common Discipline for Coventry Cathedral in these words:

So I spent a week here in May 1966. I imbibed something of the spirit of a community in which prayer has been offered under a common discipline for over twelve hundred years. I tramped the rolling Bavarian countryside and I sat, often alone, in the huge baroque basilica, interpreting the grand design of the magnificent paintings and sculptures which throng the walls and ceilings. Often my eyes would return to our own Cross of Nails in its place of honour on the central altar and sometimes an unseen organist would fill the church with glorious music, music usually of the high baroque. In the cell allotted to me I read for the first time in my life, and pondered on, the wise, humane and charitable Rule of St Benedict; also the lively, shrewd and equally charitable Rule of the Taizé Community, that fine band of brothers within the Reformed tradition who have made the unity of all Christian people the ferment of their devotion. I became convinced that amid the pressures, opportunities and problems of our work at Coventry Cathedral we, too, urgently needed a Common Discipline. Of course it would be a very different affair from the 'religious life' of monks and nuns. Our work team consists of a variety of people, about half of us clergy and half lay, about half of us married and half of us unmarried, spanning a very wide range of age and of religious conviction. Moreover, we are bound together not by a common home, that which provides the greatly treasured stabilitas, stability and security of a Benedictine community, but by the less pervasive bonds of a common work. On the other hand, I found that some of the provisions of the two Rules exactly fitted our Coventry situation. Consider this, for example, from the prologue to the Rule of St Benedict:

We have therefore to establish a school of the Lord's Service, in the setting forth of which we hope to order nothing that is harsh or rigorous. But if anything be somewhat strictly laid down, according to the dictates of sound reason, for the amendment of vices or the preservation of charity, do not therefore fly in dismay from the way of salvation whose beginning cannot but be strait and difficult.

Or this from the Rule of Taizé:

With the growing number of visitors, we run into the danger of cutting ourselves off from them, by reclusion, in order to defend ourselves. On the contrary, while preserving our deeper life, keeping a certain discernment and avoiding feverish dissipation, let us remember on every occasion how to be open and hospitable . . . People who come to us expect bread, and if we present them with stones to look at, we shall have fallen short of our ecumenical vocation. They seek in us men who radiate God. This implies a life hidden in God, so that the presence of Christ which is borne by each brother may be renewed in us.

But as both St Benedict and the Prior of Taizé would certainly wish, we have found an even greater inspiration in the Scriptures and, in particular, in St Paul's letter to the Christians in Galatia. It is an amazing testimony to the power of the Spirit in the life of the apostle that a letter which is conceived in so passionate a controversy should conclude in so charitable and penetrating an analysis of the common life. Our present Common Discipline contains three sections: the Common Discipline; Additional Voluntary Discipline; for Corporate Meditation. This third section, 'read, item by item, before breakfast on Monday mornings by the Provost', consists first of selections from St Paul's letter to the Christians in Galatia (New English Bible) and secondly of free paraphrases, adapted to our own situation, of selections from the rule of the Taizé community.

It took us about two years of consultation to fix the first form of the Common Discipline for the staff of Coventry

Cathedral. This is printed as the appendix to the Provost's book, *Basics and Variables* (Hodder and Stoughton, 1970). It contains two parts, 'The Spirit of the Discipline' and 'The Practice of the Discipline'. The former consists of a fairly full introduction which relates the Discipline to the Benedictine tradition and differentiates it from that tradition; plus the section 'For Corporate Meditation'. The second part contains the practical details, including provision for prayer and worship, work, study, recreation, holidays, sleep, food and drink, use of money, consultants, common meals, membership and revision and administration of the Discipline.

Two years later, in 1970, the Common Discipline was thoroughly revised into its present form. Meanwhile, it has been adopted (and adapted) for use by the Cathedral congregation and by the ruridecanal chapter (the local unit of clergy of the Church of England) of Coventry North. The Provost has distributed hundreds of copies in the United States and it has also been well received in Denmark and Norway as well as being translated into German and distributed by Dr Fritz Keienberg, director of the Evangelical Academy at Iserlohn. It has attracted deep interest in such widely diverse Christian communities as the historic Benedictine Abbey of Bec Hellouin (which has given to the Church in England three Archbishops of Canterbury), the parish church of Fareham in Hampshire, and the Corrymeela Community in Northern Ireland, a Christian group dedicated to works of reconciliation.

Since then this Common Discipline has been widely adopted within the Community of the Cross of Nails, an international network of over seventy Christian centres committed to a ministry of reconciliation and renewal. The Paper from which I have just extensively quoted ends with these words:

Not that I wish to leave you with a false impression of a success story such as my personal enthusiasm for this development may well have conveyed to you. Whereas on the one hand a younger colleague once told me that she did not know how she could have managed in a personal crisis without the help of her consultant, on the other hand I have reason to believe that this Common Discipline hardly impinges at all on the lives of others of us, apart from attendance at the common meals. The Common Discipline, like the sabbath before it, is made for its members and not vice versa. Its effects are largely invisible and its principle is completely adaptable to the felt needs of a very wide range of communities.

At Coventry I also became heavily involved with the Corrymeela Community in Northern Ireland, particularly in the collecting of money for their Coventry House and also to some extent in their ongoing programme. The members of this Community, both Protestant and Roman Catholic, are 'called together as a Community to be an instrument of God's peace, to serve our society and to share in the life of the Church'. (From the Commitment of Each Member of the Corrymeela Community.) It was a great privilege to take to Corrymeela a Coventry Cross of Nails and, not long afterwards to take part, with my wife, in the first residential course for school-children at Corrymeela. I have told the story of what those children taught me before (in *Life Style – A Parable of Sharing*, published by Turnstone Press, 1982), but for me it was so important a lesson that it bears repeating. I quote:

Some forty thirteen- and fourteen-year-olds from areas of special need in Belfast assembled with their teachers to study the geography of the coastal area. Half of them were from two Roman Catholic schools and the other half Protestants from two maintained schools. One Roman Catholic girl told me that she had been punched in the face by a member of a street gang of Protestant youths. A boy told me that he had on several occasions been paid fifty pence a time by IRA agents to throw stones at the soldiers. Another wrote afterwards about Corrymeela: 'At first I was afraid to go, as I thought there would be fighting. But it wasn't like that at all. We found out that they are just like us.'

Like everyone else I was given a job to do – leading an epilogue each evening. For one I had brought an Easter egg with me, the season being appropriate. An egg makes an excellent teaching aid on the theme of new life and I proposed, as the climax of my epilogue, to break it open and share it around. But it looked to me a very small egg when I called for a plate, peeled off the silver paper and broke the hollow egg in two. With a silent prayer I handed the plate to the front row, inviting everyone to break off a piece and pass it on. At the end about a third was left and we voted unanimously to give it to Anna, the Corrymeela cook. It was like a celebration of the Holy Communion. I shall never forget the simple lesson those children were teaching me that evening; that when resources are limited there is enough for everyone's need, but not enough for anyone's greed.

Other communities to which I took Coventry Crosses of Nails were Taizé in Burgundy and the Benedictine Abbey which administers the great basilica of St Paul's Outside the Walls in Rome. Taizé's twin programme of 'struggle and contemplation' and its particular appeal to the young may be well known to many readers. As I recorded in *Life Style – A Parable of Sharing* the experience of presenting the Cross of Nails to Brother Roger in the Taizé Chapel which was full to overflowing was a moving one. Less widely known is the ministry of St Paul's Outside the Walls which at that time, in the early seventies, under the exuberant leadership of Abbot Franzoni, had become an effective 'parable of sharing'.

St Paul's, for example, supported financially and with public encouragement the workers in two industries who believed themselves to have been victimised by being locked out and had retaliated by occupying their factories. As a consequence, so I was told, Neo-Fascist rowdies invaded the basilica during the Sunday Youth Mass and broke the guitars of youth choir members over their heads. At a more personal level of ministry, members of the congregation had taken into their homes mentally disturbed adolescents found too violent by their own parents to be received back home during or after treatment.

St Paul's 'parable of sharing' extended beyond a concern for the *exclusi*, the 'dropped out' – a more accurate designation than 'drop outs' – of their own city. In the weeks before the Bangladeshi war of liberation the Abbot called the community and the congregation to a fortnight of fasting and prayer. In the light of this corporate commitment and the reflections that derived from it, he sent an appeal for certain specific actions to the Indian, Pakistani and Italian governments. One of the monks told me that abbots of St Paul's had always been consecrated as bishops on their appointment, *honoris causa*. Abbot Franzoni, however, had caused many a raised eyebrow in the Vatican establishment by refusing this honour on the proper ground that a bishop's job was to be the chief pastor of his diocesan flock and that it was wrong to use this holy office as a means of conferring status or prestige.

At Coventry Cathedral we had a number of opportunities of meeting the variously disadvantaged, sharing their experience and learning from them. To me the most interesting part of my own work as education officer was the organisation of residential courses for students and for senior school pupils at Kennedy House, our forty-bedded youth centre. The most popular of these courses were variations on the theme of 'Life in a Modern City'. The method was experiential, the instruction being built round visits to various groups in the city. One of the most effective was to one of the Sikh temples, something that in those days was rather out of the ordinary. We would usually have a lecture, with slides, on Sikhism, the evening before the visit and instruct the students that during the visit they would have to cover their heads, take off their shoes and also accept whatever they were offered by way of food and drink. For it is a Sikh custom to offer such hospitality to all who visit their temples. The visit was invariably enjoyed and the students impressed by the dignity and friendliness of their hosts and hostesses and by the spirituality of their faith.

On our return to Kennedy House we would usually have a session of reflection and discussion on such subjects as how best to welcome and support such ethnic minorities and also how best to conduct the interfaith dialogue. In this way hundreds of young people received a sympathetic introduction to a significant group of their fellow citizens.

IN BRISTOL

In 1975 we moved to Bristol. In 1983 I prepared a Paper for a consultation at Bristol Cathedral with a visiting group from the Marktkirche, Hannover, entitled 'Our Cathedrals – Solidarity with the poor and the oppressed?' This was subsequently published in *Cathedral*, the English cathedrals' journal. The question mark in the title is deliberate. For as I wrote in the introductory paragraph:

> The subject looks distinctly unpromising. Our splendid buildings make inordinate demands on the financial and manpower resources of most of us. Our equally splendid style of choral worship is not only very costly in itself but also tends to attract a regular congregation whose corporate priority is unlikely to be a whole-hearted political and moral commitment to the poor and the oppressed. On the other hand, cathedrals can become without too much difficulty a kind of natural habitat for those who wish to articulate the voice of the voiceless, prisoners of conscience, ethnic minorities, the unemployed, the aged, victims of sexism, the hungry poor.

I went on to give four examples of 'selected case histories':

In 1974 Bristol Cathedral Chapter observed that whereas most if not all dioceses have one or more Youth Chaplains, no diocese to our knowledge had a Chaplain to the Older Generation. Yet the percentage of senior citizens in our population continues to grow. Many of them are oppressed by financial, mental or physical disabilities while many others are fit and alert and longing to put their neglected skills to good use. So we appointed a part-time Chaplain to the Older Generation. She quickly built up an ecumenical community of over a hundred people to whom she has ministered materially and spiritually and for whom she has provided at the Cathedral a congenial meeting place and lunch club.

In 1976 a joint choir of adult members of Bristol Cathedral and Clifton (Roman Catholic) Cathedral choirs was invited to sing in Calcutta by the late Canon Subir Biswas in charge of St Paul's (Church of North India) Cathedral there. They sang not only at services in the cathedral and in a large Roman Catholic church but also in one of Mother Teresa's homes, in Old People's Homes, at an Indian music centre and, after leaving Calcutta, in the gardens of Fatehpur Sikri and the Taj Mahal. Canon Biswas himself supplied the *raison d'être* of this unusual adventure: 'Calcutta is one of the world's great cities. Its people deserve the best. English cathedral music is the best. Therefore you must come.'

In 1983 two incidents may be selected for comment. On May 28 a group of unemployed men and women, on a protest march from Land's End to London, paused in Bristol to join in a special service at our cathedral. This had been requested by Mr Ron Nethercott, regional secretary of the Transport and General Workers Union. Our bishop specially broke into his sabbatical to attend, and other denominations supplied a choir, a soloist, readers of Scripture and a leader for the intercessions. One local MP was in the congregation of several hundred people, but another wrote to me to protest that such a service was an inappropriate political act. Afterwards one marcher told me: 'I am not a Christian, but that was the most moving experience I have ever had in my life.'

Shortly afterwards the sponsors of the Argentina

Reconciliation Fund announced the fund's closure after it had topped the £3,000 mark. After the Falklands war a small group of Bristol Christians called on me to ask for help in setting up this fund for the widows and orphans of Argentinian conscripts killed in battle and for others disabled in the fighting. The Bristol Council of Christian Churches, whose office, like that of Christian Aid, is on our premises was able to give them essential back-up and the World Council of Churches undertook to channel the funds to the right quarter.

I concluded the article or Paper with a section on 'And one that went wrong', of which the central paragraph read as follows:

Bristol Cathedral School has very close historic links with the cathedral. Our choristers attend there for example. Under the chairmanship of my predecessor the school governors, faced in the early seventies with the probability that the direct grant would be withdrawn if a Labour government came to power, had worked hard in drawing up three options in that event. The first was that the school should become voluntary aided and serve the inner city. This option was unanimously adopted by a resolution of the Chapter. The consequences of its implementation would have been far-reaching. The deprived inner city would have had a first-class secondary school of its own. As for the cathedral, half its choristers would probably by now have been drawn from ethnic minorities and the whole social character of its community radically diversified. But the Chapter's decision was taken against the advice of the headmaster at the time and most of the teaching staff. A large majority of the parents were up in arms against it. What proved decisive against it, however, was the reorganisation of local government. The new Avon County Council became the local education authority and decided to oppose the scheme. The governors had little option but to go independent.

The reader can imagine that we had some problems explaining all that to our friends from Hannover. But this last example may serve to illustrate how difficult it can be for the institutional church to express in its life style the desired solidarity with the poor. The Church of England is often at a distinct disadvantage at this point, compared with the Free Churches on the one hand and the Roman Catholic Church on the other. The Methodist Church in particular has an excellent record of siding with the poor and the oppressed. With reference to the particular point at issue it is interesting to observe that the great majority of the Roman Catholic direct grant schools became voluntary aided while the great majority of those associated with the Church of England went independent. Individual Christians, however, are not bound to the cultural ethos of their particular denomination nor even to that of the institutional Church as a whole. We are free to adopt a personal life style of some solidarity with the poor (unless we are poor ourselves – in which case we are not free to do anything else). If we do so, however, we must realise that we are swimming against a great tide of consumerist culture. In Australia once my wife and I were being interviewed on this subject on the local (commercial) television.

'Well, what actual things ought you to do without if you adopt your ideas?' the interviewer asked. The answer ought to have come pat. 'Well, anything advertised on television for a start.' On the other hand, a few days later, a tough reporter from the *Sydney Sun* closed his notebook with the words: 'Well, all this is just what Jesus taught, I reckon.'

5

FOR TODAY AND TOMORROW

The testimony of the Bible and the testimony of Christian tradition refer inevitably to events and experiences in the past. Even the chapter of personal testimony refers to the recent past. But it is a Christian life style for the present and for the future that we have in mind in this book. So I must now try to answer the question why a disciplined life style which expresses solidarity with the poor and the oppressed is particularly relevant now and in the immediate future. To do this I have to begin briefly with the Scriptures again.

THE KINGDOM OF GOD AND HIS RIGHTEOUSNESS

According to St Matthew's Gospel Jesus ended the most specific paragraph about simplicity of life style in all His teaching with the words: 'But seek first his [i.e. God's] kingdom and his righteousness, and all these things shall be yours as well' (Matt. 6:33). It is well understood that both these ideas (which are more than mere ideas), God's kingdom and God's righteousness, have both a personal and a social reference. God's kingdom, 'on earth as it is in heaven' (6:10), means His kingly rule both throughout His creation and in particular over His human family, and also within each one of us personally. To this kingdom, God's righteousness is the key. This word 'righteousness', *dikaiosunē* in Greek, carries the meaning, first, of God's own merciful judgment, then also both of the justice which He wills between the members of His family and of the justification before Him which He gives us personally by grace through faith. What in this world prevents the fuller realisation of God's kingdom and His righteousness both at the social or global level and at the personal level is that covetousness which is forbidden in the tenth commandment. This covetousness is also identified by St Paul with the idolatry which is forbidden in the first commandment (Col. 3:5). A Christian life style which promotes justice within the human family and is free from covetousness, avarice or greed is as relevant now and in the future as it has ever been.

In the early years of the nineteenth century the bells of the city churches of Bristol where I live used to ring out in triumph whenever a Bill to abolish the slave trade was defeated in Parliament. As we look back on our Christian forebears we are tempted to amazement at their insensitivity on this issue. We wonder how they could have been so blind to the horrors of so infamous a trade. If human kind safely reaches, say, the year 2100, will they not look back on us with a similar amazement and wonder at how we tolerated a world in which up to a thousand million fellow members of the family were allowed to live in such abject poverty while a substantial minority practised an extravagant style of life which was hundreds of times more prodigal in the expenditure of the Earth's resources? Let us not be misled. The cruelty of this injustice is as foul as that of the slave trade, but on a much larger scale. In my previous book, *Life Style – A Parable of Sharing*, I quote these words of Jill Tweedie, writing in the *Guardian* (Nov 11th, 1974):

I had imagined, in my unforgivable ignorance, that starvation like great cold, after the first agonising pains, lulled you to a death disguised as apathy and sleep. Horribly this is not so.

Pain takes its toll to the last, starvation is torture. Kerato-malacia turns children's eyes to blank marbles. B2 de-ficiencies strip the tongue of its surface, burn the lips, ulcer the mouth and with hideous irony, make swallowing difficult. C deficiencies cause bleeding gums, loosening teeth, multiple haemorrhages. Children without vitamin D have gross de-formations of the bones, without vitamin K bleed with no coagulation. Lack of nicotinic acid produces pellagra, a red-ness like sunburn that ends in great purple eruptions. Kwashiorkor blows up children's stomachs to grotesque balloons, dwindles their limbs to sticks. In all under-nourishment infection is a constant threat and, eventually, the body ceases to function and death ensues – but only after prolonged vomiting and diarrhoea.

I once quoted these terrible words at an open-air meeting. The next day one of those present, an old-age pensioner, came to me and counted out ten ten-pound notes into my hand. 'For the starving,' she said simply. She may well have taken a sizeable step forward in realising her responsibility, what Rex Ambler has called 'structural understanding'.

He writes (in a broadsheet published by One for Chris-tian Renewal):

When I reach that level of awareness, I have what we might call a structural understanding of myself and the world. We can distinguish this from the more naïve, personal under-standing which is the awareness of every day life. The differ-ence between these levels of understanding emerges more sharply when we consider the kind of action they lead to. Take for example our relation to the poor of the world. We can perceive this in two different ways. With 'naïve, personal' understanding we can see the poor as groups of unfortunate people who demand our sympathy and compassion. They may live a long way off and belong to another nation and another religion, but we can still choose to regard them as neighbours. The appropriate action is to reach out a hand to help them. But with a 'structural understanding' we can see the poor as made poor by our own pursuit of wealth. We may have no individual contact at all, or even the possibility of such. We can none the less be aware that our manner of Western life is possible for us only because we in the West, collectively, can rely on the vast resources of cheap labour in the poorer countries. We cannot now choose to have relations with the poor. We already have relations, structural relations, which happen also to be unjust relations. The appropriate action is to redress the balance of power and justice by paying attention first of all to our manner of life in the West.

SOLIDARITY WITH ALL GOD'S CREATURES

As we 'pay attention first of all to our manner of life in the West' we do well to sit at the feet of our Asian, African and Latin American brothers and sisters. Here is 'A New Creed', composed by the late Subir Biswas, formerly canon in charge of St Paul's Cathedral, Calcutta:

We believe in one WORLD, full of riches meant for everyone to enjoy.
We believe in one RACE – the family of humankind, learning to live together by the way of self-sacrifice.
We believe in one LIFE, exciting and positive,
Which enjoys all beauty, integrity and science,
Uses the discipline of work to enrich society, harmonises with the life of Jesus and develops into total happiness.

We believe in one morality – LOVE,
The holiness of sharing the sorrows and joys of others,
Of bringing people together as true friends,
Of working to get rid of the causes of poverty, injustice, ignorance and fear;
LOVE, the test of all our thoughts and motives:
LOVE, which is God forgiving us, accepting us, and making us confident under His Holy Spirit's control.

We believe in JESUS, and the Bible's evidence about Him,

Whose life, death, and resurrection prove God's permanent
   love for the world,
Who combines in Himself life, love, truth, humanity, reality
   and God,
Saving, guiding, reforming and uniting all people who follow
   His way.

We believe in the PURPOSE OF GOD
To unite in Christ everything, spiritual and secular,
To bring about constructive revolution in society, individuals
   and nations
And to establish world government under His fatherly
   direction.'

In writing of 'one world' and 'one life' as well as of 'one
race' and 'one morality' Subir Biswas transcended the
merely human dimension. So must our Christian life style.
We are called to a simplicity of life not only for the sake
of our fellow members of the human family but also
in solidarity with all God's creatures. Consider this
anonymous 'prayer of the tree':

You who pass by and would raise your hand against me,
   hearken ere you harm me,
I am the heat of your hearth on the cold winter night, the
   friendly shade screening you from summer sun,
And my fruits are refreshing draughts quenching your thirst
   as you journey on.
I am the beam that holds your house, the board of your table,
   the bed on which you lie, the timber that builds your boat.
I am the handle of your hoe, the door of your homestead, the
   wood of your cradle, the shell of your last resting place.
I am the gift of God and the friend of man.
You who pass by, listen to my prayer, HARM ME NOT.

Our responsibility towards the fellow members of our
human family and that towards other living creatures may
be distinguished but not entirely separated. Thus the
massive deforestation of the Amazon basin to provide,

among other things, huge beef cattle ranches may well be a decisive factor in the climatic changes that are bringing perennial droughts to the Sahel area in Africa. It may even be having a permanently deleterious effect on the whole global climate. On a smaller scale the destruction of forests in Zimbabwe to provide fuel to dry the tobacco crop deprives subsistence farmers and their families of the domestic fuel they need for cooking. The whole ecology of the planet is as interdependent (and fragile) as is its economy.

These are insights for today and for tomorrow, neither as fully realised by previous generations nor as urgent for them. We have entered a new era, in which our human destiny is to conserve and share our planet's resources, not to continue to increase our exploitation and consumption of them.

This point was well made in a meditation by the Norfolk naturalist, Ted Ellis, which was read at a special service in Norwich Cathedral for World Wildlife Year:

We give thanks, O God, for the gift of Life on this earth: for all life. Thy mysteries surround us, in the depths of Space and the eternity of Time. The sunshine and the rainbow delight our eyes. In the peace of a starry night and in the shadow of the mountain we are aware of Thy presence. Our senses are comforted by the sweet distillations of flowers; our hearts are warmed by kinship with Man and Nature. Cold and heat, storm and calm, darkness and light, diversify our pilgrimage. Our spirits ebb and flow like the tides of the ocean and waves upon the shore; but to our consciousness of elemental things is added, in Mankind, a spirit of reflection and forethought, whereby we gave gained stewardship of this world of ancient wealth and living wonder.

As we pause now to consider our involvement in the destiny of this glorious inheritance, let us resolve that our works henceforth may be attuned to the music that springs from our hearts in thankfulness for Thy great mercies.

In our selfishness and arrogance we have betrayed Thy trust. In our demands for luxury we have neglected the starving, wasted Thy gifts and sullied the pure air, the rivers and the seas. As we gather to ourselves the bounty of the earth, we weigh not the consequences. We isolate ourselves in pride and defiance of Thy perfect Law. We molest our fellow men and destroy the Eden of Thy creation as locusts lay waste a green land.

All of us who are gathered in this sanctuary are to some extent aware of our collective failure to honour the code of life which Thou hast set before us. We pray that we may reject what is evil and that we may discipline our actions henceforth to the furtherance of Thy design, with humility, understanding and compassion.

In our awareness of and conformity to the insights that are appropriate to the new era, Christians should be to the fore.

Should Christians do their own thing, living in a style different from their neighbours? In recent years a movement has appeared which says: yes . . . the true picture is of individuals finding their own integrity. . . . This seems to be a genuine renewal in the story of the Christian Church as a body guided by the Holy Spirit; and incidentally it takes us back to the earliest days, when Christianity certainly was highly distinctive.

So wrote David Edwards, now Provost of Southwark, in an article for *Mowbrays Journal* (Autumn, 1976). That distinctiveness of the early Christians to which he refers was finely described by St Cyprian in the third century:

This seems a cheerful world, Donatus, when I view it from this fair garden, under the shadow of these vines. But if I climbed some great mountain and looked out over the wide lands, you know very well what I would see. Brigands on the high road, pirates on the seas, in the amphitheatres men murdered to please the applauding crowds, under all roofs misery and selfishness. It is really a bad world, Donatus, an incredibly bad world. Yet in the midst of it I have found a quiet and holy people. They have discovered a joy which is a thousand times better than any pleasure of this sinful life. They are despised and persecuted, but they care not. They have overcome the world. These people, Donatus, are the Christians . . . and I am one of them.

Today – and tomorrow – Christians are still called to a distinctive life style. We may rejoice, however, that certain broad features of this life style are shared with those of other faiths or of none.

In African traditional religion the names given to God indicate a monotheistic faith in one God who is the source of all being. From this stems a sense of justice and a strong feeling of community. Widows and orphans are specially cared for and the community extends even beyond death to include ancestors who are honoured and live close to God. This faith gave stability to African society, but it was discounted, its value distorted and in some cases totally destroyed by the impact of conquest and colonisation.

The vision of Hinduism is one of the indwelling of the Lord as the self (*atman*) of all beings. In and through every living thing we can perceive and worship Him. Each one therefore possesses a unique and intrinsic dignity from which nothing can detract. . . .

In the eyes of Buddhists all are equal, irrespective of colour or creed. The basic recognition of human rights is therefore integral to Buddhism. Freedom and justice are like the very air human beings breathe. Life without them is like a country without a spring: nothing grows or flourishes there. The righteous way and the method of non-violence are for Buddhists the way of achieving equality in social, economic and political life, and eventually achieving the good of humanity.

Jews, Christians and Muslims all agree that human beings are made in the image of God and share a common human lineage. Human conduct must be based on the sanctity of human life and sense of human community . . . The prophets of Israel, the Lord Jesus Christ and the Holy Prophet Muhammed all called for justice for the poor and oppressed and spoke of the judgment of God against those who did not act justly.

This quotation from the 1984 Declaration of the Inter-Faith Colloquium on Apartheid can be read as referring not only to the injustice of apartheid but to the whole great weight of injustice against the poor and the oppressed. Nor is it only believers who are called to a life style of sharing and of solidarity. Such a life style, today and tomorrow, is a sign of being fully human.

Four main points have already emerged to justify the conviction that a life style of solidarity with the oppressed is especially required today and tomorrow. The first is our contemporary understanding of the global scale of the injustice that infests human society. The second is our contemporary understanding of the structural relationship between the rich and the poor. The third is our contemporary understanding that this structural relationship of interdependence extends even beyond the confines of the human family to the whole created universe, in particular to all living creatures. The fourth is our contemporary understanding that people of all faiths and of none share a common vocation to live simply that all may simply live. Together these four understandings amount to a new era of thought and action, a new age of enlightenment in which we are beginning to realise that our corporate destiny for the next few centuries is to conserve where formerly we exploited, to share where formerly we took for ourselves.

OUR GREED DENIES THEIR NEED

A fifth essential contemporary understanding has to be of the extent of our own greed, avarice or covetousness 'which is idolatry' (Col. 3:5). I shall content myself with two examples, the one personal and the other public; how we spend Christmas on the one hand and the international arms trade on the other.

On December 21st, 1982, at a time of alleged economic recession, the *Guardian* published an article by Martin Walker entitled 'An 18-carat Christmas'.

At Harrods they call it the year of the pearl, with the biggest demand for necklaces in the £1,500–£2,000 range. And towards the bottom of the price range, they cannot get enough of their champagne-flavoured toothpaste (£1.95) and gold-plated toothbrushes (£3.75). And that is on top of their 120 tons of Christmas pudding, 17 tons of fresh turkey, 13 tons of Stilton cheese, 11 tons of chocolate, 2½ tons of nuts, ½ ton of caviar, and (at the last count) 21,595 tubes of indigestion tablets . . . Harrods claims a bumper year for wine, with its quadruple magnum of champagne at £115 selling by the case, and something of a run on the 1966 Château Petrus (£125 a bottle). It claims to have sold 'lots' of their top-of-the-range £1,000 hampers while Fortnum and Mason has sold but one. But Fortnum's £550 hamper is their best-seller with some paying the extra postage to get them to the Falkland Islands in time.

By contrast here are 'Ten questions for Christmas', thought up by the members of a cell of the Life Style Movement in the United States:

How would you celebrate Christmas if you had no money to spend on gifts?

What could you do for your parents, relatives and friends that would be a gift of yourself?

What gifts can you make using natural and recyclable materials?

How can we help some people whom we may not even know, be glad to be alive at Christmas?

How would Jesus want his birthday celebrated?

Is there something we can make together as a family that would have real meaning for us? Or something special a parent could make for a child as a surprise?

Have you ever thought about sharing a talent of yours (music, speech, a skit) as a gift?

What in the past has meant the most to you at Christmas?

How can our celebration focus more on people than on things?

Do children really expect as many presents at Christmas as we think we should give them?

Vast as is the profligacy associated with our celebration of Christmas – how ironic it is, considering the nature of the event we are celebrating – it pales into insignificance when we turn to my example of public profligacy, the arms trade. The figures keep escalating. But for decades now they have been beyond the imagination of most of us.

Between 1978 and 1982 worldwide expenditure on arms quadrupled to some six hundred thousand million pounds, about thirty times the amount spent on Development Aid. Today one tank costs about as much as four thousand tons of rice. The cost of one jet plane approximates to that of forty thousand village pharmacies. Allocation of the cost of one Trident-carrying submarine would enable the World Health Office to eradicate malaria and river blindness from the world. Even in peace-time the United States armed forces consume as much oil as the whole of Southern Asia, two thirds as much as the whole of Africa.

Now it has been argued that the arms trade must be maintained, even increased because of the quarter of a million people in Britain alone who are employed in the manufacture and distribution of arms. Those of us whose employment is more or less secure must not minimise this problem. But the solution of it surely lies elsewhere than in the continued production of these useless and dangerous products. The long-term solution, if there is one, lies in a massive increase in the purchasing power of the very poor throughout the world so that they will be able to buy a greatly increased volume of useful goods and services from the industrialised nations. Short-term we have the example of the shop stewards' committee at Lucas Aerospace who drew up a list of over a hundred alternative products which could replace the already declining arms contracts.

It has also been argued that there is no direct connection between the arms trade and world poverty. That may be the case. But I believe that it remains true that, in President Eisenhower's words: 'Every gun that is made, every warship launched, every rocket fired, signifies in a final sense, a theft from those who hunger and are not fed, from those who are cold and are not clothed.'

The attempt is also made to exclude nuclear arms from this discussion since not many of these are sold by one country to another. However they do take up a great deal of labour, capital and, above all, scientific and technological skill in their manufacture and deployment. The cost of a single Trident submarine, for example, would give a year's schooling to no less than sixteen million poor children in Asia and Africa. Moreover, the continuing manufacture and deployment of these appalling weapons can achieve no military purpose. As another military leader of great distinction, the late Earl Mountbatten, has said (in May 1979 at Strasbourg): 'The nuclear arms race has no military purpose. Wars cannot be fought with nuclear weapons. Their existence only adds to our perils because of the illusions they have generated.'

AN IDEA WHOSE TIME HAS COME

As we contemplate the monstrous proliferation of nuclear weapons and the threat which they pose to the survival of the human family we may surely conclude that never before in human history has there been so urgent a need for an alternative way of living, a life style of voluntary simplicity. Of course this 'idea whose time has come' has been taken up by Christians and others in various ways. I shall conclude this chapter with a few representative examples.

In 1974 in a message sent to the UN Secretary-General on the occasion of a special session of the UN General Assembly, Pope Paul declared: 'We appeal to the developed nations to make great efforts to forgo their own immediate advantages, and to adopt a new life style that will exclude both excessive consumption and those superfluous needs that are often artificially engendered.'

In 1980 Christian Aid issued a leaflet entitled 'Thoughts about Life Style', which included the following paragraphs:

Live more simply that all of us may simply live.

That's attractive, simple logic, but is it really as simple as that?

The poor here and in the Third World won't automatically benefit because we choose to live more simply . . .

One man's simplicity may be another man's luxury.

It's all a matter of degree. There are no easy answers.

Christian Aid describes itself as a partnership with the poor. If we are serious about our commitment to the poor we can't live extravagant lives.

Simpler living is:

– a sign of our own integrity;

– a sign that we mean business when we say we care about the poor;

– a sign that we are prepared to do something. And we'll almost certainly be happier too, if we live more simply.

There seems to be no stopping an idea whose time has come. More and more people are becoming more and more aware of the urgent need to share the resources of our planet more equitably among the members of the human family and to conserve them for future generations.

It is better to reduce our consumption of valuable resources voluntarily than to be forced to make reductions because of future scarcities.

So more and more people are thinking about and taking action over:

- the food they eat and the food they grow;
- the clothes they wear;
- the way they feed their pets;
- the transport they use for work and leisure;
- saving energy by good insulation;
- avoiding waste;
- urging change in patterns of world trade through political campaigning.

LIFE STYLE is part of the exploration for responsible ways of living.

LIFE STYLE isn't about giving up this or that, or saying that the problem is too big and we can't do anything.

LIFE STYLE is more about thinking individually and together what we can do and then making the necessary adjustments in our lives . . .

LIFE STYLE is about asking the right questions rather than adopting easy solutions.

LIFE STYLE is about quality of life rather than standard of living.

LIFE STYLE is about our attitudes as well as our actions.

LIFE STYLE helps us to realise that the poor have vital resources – spiritual, moral, human resources – to share with us.

LIFE STYLE is a way of continuous concern for the poor.

LIFE STYLE for the Christian is part of being a disciple of the God who calls us to follow Him by sharing with our fellow men.

LIFE STYLE is about seeking what is really worthwhile, and discovering some basis of hope for a more humane future.

Will you think about
- your own life style?
- your church's life style?
- the nation's life style?

Will you match your thoughts with action?

The Taizé Community is another Christian body which has greatly concerned itself with a sharing life style. Under the heading 'Sharing' a writer in the *Taizé Newsletter* declares:

As a result of their deep fellowship, the first Christians shared everything with one another (Acts 2:42–6).

Sharing involves both giving and receiving, in joy, simplicity, humility and spontaneity (Luke 12:33–4).

Sharing also means identifying ourselves with those who suffer (Heb. 10:34).

What can I share? What am I already sharing with others today? What else could I share?

What can others share with me?

Who am I in solidarity with? What concrete ways can we find of being in solidarity with the excluded?

What experiences of group sharing have I had (for example at home, at school, at work, in church)?

What difficulties do I find in sharing? How can they be overcome?

Sharing means simplifying our lives, leaving aside all that is not essential, all that is superfluous. Sharing means putting the Beatitudes into practice (Matt. 5:1–12).

What is vital to me? What can I leave aside or give up in order to make my life a life for others?

What is my scale of values? In what or in whom do I place my confidence?

Who or what can help me discover what is superfluous in my life?

Where can I find support in times of discouragement?

What ways exist of sharing not only with those who are close by but also with those in need who are far away?

How can I turn my home, or my church, into a place of hospitality, peace and forgiveness? To help me in this, do there already exist in my area tiny oases where struggle and contemplation, prayer and daily life are brought together, which can serve as a reference point?

Do I know people who have made their lives into a 'parable of sharing'?

What can I do to share something of my life with those who have chosen a direction that is opposite to mine, with those who do not think like me, with women and men of other continents, with people of all ages?

How can we take part in a transformation of the structures of society in order to build a society founded on sharing?'

Having begun this section with a quotation from Pope Paul and continued with full references to two well-known ecumenical bodies, Christian Aid and the Taizé Community, I should add that those in the evangelical tradition have not been behindhand. Under the heading 'Simplify Life style and end injustice, say Evangelicals', the Ecumenical Press Service reported as follows:

Hoddesdon, UK – A strong challenge to Christians in affluent circumstances to simplify their lifestyle and take political action to bring about radical change in the present unjust trade and economic structures is contained in a statement from the first International Consultation on Simple Life style held here late March.

The Consultation was sponsored jointly by the Lausanne Theology and Education Group of the Lausanne Committee on World Evangelisation, and the Unit on Ethics and Society of the Theology Commission of the World Evangelical Fellowship.

The statement is described as representing the strongest call yet by Evangelical Christians to take a stand against economic injustice and in support of a redistribution of wealth.

'Poverty and excessive wealth, militarism and the arms industry, and the unjust distribution of capital, land and resources are issues of power and powerlessness,' the statement says. 'Without a shift of power through structural change, these problems cannot be solved.'

The statement prefaces its call for evangelical involvement in changing international structures with a commitment to responsible stewardship, freedom from 'the seduction of riches', a new sense of community among believers, and personal and corporate life style.

Meanwhile as early as 1970 at their conference at Nottingham University 450 members of the Church Missionary Society made certain affirmations, including the following:

A style of living that tells is one in which simplicity rules, questions are openly faced and Christ is seen, working in the world as his Father works.

It is a life marked by repentance, hope and joy and lived in the Spirit, in response to a changing world marked by solidarity with all men and a longing for their wholeness, and a concern for the right use of God's creation.

Prayer is at the heart of this style of living giving man a resource and a goal.

For this we need to reawaken in men the sense of awe and wonder. We need to use the arts and to learn from other cultures.

The Christian style of living is response to God's love, faith working through love, which means evangelism in the context of service.

'FORTY FOUR HORSE-WAGGON LOADS'

Finally may I lighten this properly rather earnest little catalogue of contemporary or near contemporary statements on a Christian life style for today and tomorrow by a further reference to the Christian tradition, this time in the person of Canon Sydney Smith (1771–1845) who was for a time a canon of our cathedral in Bristol where I work. On September 29th, 1843, he wrote to his friend, J. A. Murray, as follows:

You are, I hear, attending more to diet than heretofore. If you wish for anything like happiness in the fifth act of life, eat and drink about one half of what you *could* eat and drink. Did I ever tell you my calculation about eating and drinking? Having ascertained the weight of what I could live upon so as to preserve health and strength, and what I did live upon, I found that, betweeen ten and seventy years of age, I had eaten and drunk forty four-horse waggon loads of meat and drink more than would have preserved me in life and health! The value of this mass of nourishment I considered to be worth seven thousand pounds sterling. It occurred to me that I must, by my voracity, have starved to death fully a hundred persons. This is a frightful calculation, but irresistibly true: and I think, dear Murray, your waggons would require an additional horse each!

6

THE LIFE STYLE COMMITMENT

JUDGE NOT THAT YOU BE NOT JUDGED

I have told elsewhere (in *Life Style – A Parable of Sharing*, chapter V) in some detail the history of the Life Style Movement from its foundation in 1972 to the time of writing that book (1981). So I shall not repeat that history here. Suffice it to say that since then I have been succeeded as the Movement's central co-ordinator by Dr John West, formerly a lecturer in metallurgy at Sheffield University. He has taken the opportunity of early retirement and so is able to give more time and energy to Life Style.

Under his leadership the Movement is grappling with a number of contemporary issues as my next chapter shows. To this end we have brought together a 'think tank' of experts in various fields. A main means of communication within the Movement is our quarterly *Newsletter* which is sent to all our members. Recently several distinguished churchmen have indicated their support, including the Bishops of Gloucester and Lincoln, the Rev. Rupert Davies, the Rev. Dr Kenneth Greet and the Rt Rev. Lesslie Newbigin.

Life Style has also become more closely associated with the Basic Communities' movement in the shape of the Little Gidding Community. Our hon. treasurer, the

Rev. Robert Van der Weyer, and our general secretary, Mrs Margaret Smith, are both members of this community. This close association of the Life Style Movement with specifically Christian people and organisations has not however deflected us from our intention and policy to remain open to people of any faith or none. The issues with which the Movement is involved are human issues, too universal to allow a sectarian approach. I made this point in our *Newsletter* (June 11th, 1984) as follows:

. . . our Life Style Movement is in line with the Christian Faith. Because Christians believe that Christ died for all, they cannot avoid a personal commitment to care for and share with all. Because Jesus was a poor man, an Asian villager in fact, and chose to remain so, Christians are called by God to cherish the poor, the dispossessed and the disadvantaged. I am convinced that we have to express our solidarity with the poor by some attempt to live more simply that all of us, the whole human family, may simply live.

Christians, however, also believe that all human beings are made in the image of God. It follows that it is truly human to share and to care. Neither Christians, therefore, nor any other group of people dare lay exclusive claim to a truly human life style. Indeed any honest Christian will joyfully acknowledge that many who do not share their beliefs challenge those who do by the superior quality of their life style. From the start, therefore, Life Style has been open to all who are willing to sign our Commitment, whatever their brand of belief, ideology or agnosticism. It follows, of course, that the Commitment is carefully worded to reflect this openness. I have myself taken every opportunity to make this clear.

So I hope that we Christian members of Life Style, especially when we find ourselves in a majority at a conference or meeting, will be sensitive to the sensibilities of those who do not share our beliefs. I hope, too, that these latter will be glad that their own participation in an idea whose time has come is shared by so many Christian friends. Within the Church it is sadly ironic that institutions whose purpose is to be foci of unity, the Order of Bishops, for example, or the Holy

Communion, have proved divisive. There is absolutely no need
for such divisions in our Life Style Movement. Let Jesus of
Nazareth have the last word: 'Judge not, and you will not be
judged ' (Luke 6:37).

This quotation is apposite also to another potential tension
within our Movement; that between the more austere
practitioners of a simple life style and the less austere.
Some of us think that it would be incompatible with our
Commitment to own a car, a deep freeze, a television.
Others abjure private education and private medicine. But
our Commitment refuses to make judgments on such
matters. Every member must decide for himself or herself. I have already referred to a similar problem in the
Rule of St Augustine. As men and women entered the
Augustinian Orders from a wide variety of social backgrounds it was found impossible to demand of each an
exact equality of life style. What would appear as extreme
simplicity of life to one might seem very secure and
comfortable to another.

THE COMMITMENT

Since *Life Style – A Parable of Sharing* was published our
Commitment has been revised once and is, at the time of
writing, in process of revision a second time. What follows
now is a current draft both of our Commitment and of the
accompanying Guidelines, together with a commentary. I
know of no better way of conveying the spirit of our
Movement.

The Life Style Movement offers a voluntary common discipline to those who are committed to a more equitable distribution of the earth's resources and to the conservation and
development of those resources for our own and future
generations.

This introduction to our Commitment sets its aim firmly in the field of social justice, conservation and world development. We believe these three causes to be closely interrelated and immediately urgent. The words 'voluntary common discipline' derive historically from my own experience of writing the original text of the Coventry Cathedral Common Discipline whose revised form underlies the international Community of the Cross of Nails. A 'common discipline' is made necessary by the powerful pressures on us to succumb to an extravagant and consumerist style of life. The word 'discipline' may not be all that popular in an age in which many of the conventional and traditional restraints upon our moral freedom have been so largely withdrawn. Yet it is precisely in such an age that self-discipline becomes the more important. We have preferred the word 'discipline' to 'rule'. On the one hand the latter implies a tighter commitment than we envisage. On the other hand it has similar disadvantages to those which St Paul discovered in the Law. A rule which we fail to keep as we live out our lives in the secular world becomes a burden of guilt.

> Recognising that the peaceful development and perhaps the survival of the human race are threatened by:
> 1. the injustice of extremes of poverty and wealth;
> 2. the profligate use of natural resources and the pollution of the environment;
> 3. the denial of useful and creative work to many people.

This section of our Commitment briefly sets out the facts (or some of them) on the basis of which such a Commitment has become urgently necessary. These facts imply a structural relationship between their poverty and our wealth. Our profligate use of the planet's generous but limited resources and the destruction of these resources by industrial pollution contribute to the denial of these resources to the poor. Under these circumstances many of the latter have no useful or creative work to do while others have to work long hours under inhumane conditions for a pittance. To recognise these facts is the first step. But it must lead to action.

> I therefore seek to:
> Live more simply that all of us may simply live;
> Give more freely that others may be free to give;
> Avoid wasteful use of resources and show care for the environment;
> Work with others for social justice through appropriate political action;
> Enjoy such good things as are compatible with this commitment.

First comes what has become the slogan of our Movement, widely borrowed by our friends and allies in the development agencies. In its original form it read: 'Live more simply that others may simply live.' We changed it after someone pointed out at a conference in the United States that we were all in the same boat, spaceship Earth, and that the survival of all depended on a more equitable distribution of this Earth's resources. Members of the Life Style Movement believe that this sentence encapsulates an idea whose time has come and which therefore has to prevail.

'Give more freely that others may be free to give.'

Living more simply is not an end in itself. In order that all of us may simply live resources must be freely shared. In the modern world the main means of realising such a sharing is by the transfer of money from the rich to the poor both by individuals and by governments. The form of this part of our Commitment is at least partly conditioned by an incident which occurred when an ecumenical choir from Bristol and Clifton (Roman Catholic) cathedrals visited Calcutta in 1976, as has already been mentioned.

All our members took part, as we were able, in the work

of St Paul's Cathedral's relief service. Clare was allotted to 'Operation Twilight'. Each evening as darkness fell a jeep left the cathedral full of food parcels to be distributed to the hungry. This was not as simple a matter as might first appear. Some of the pavement dwellers in Calcutta have jobs and therefore food. Not every poor man or woman is actually hungry. So enquiries have to be made. I asked Clare the next morning how it had gone. She told me that when they had one parcel left they approached an old man lying on the pavement. His thin body was covered only by a torn loin-cloth. They offered him the parcel. 'No,' he said, 'I have eaten today. There is someone just round the corner who has not. Give it to him.'

Calcutta Cathedral's relief service is partly financed by Christian Aid and other Western agencies. By giving to them we will have helped to enable that old man himself to make a gift that was profoundly acceptable to God. I believe that he was thereby enabled not only to affirm his human dignity but also to become one of those who, as Jesus promised, come from the East and from the West and sit down in the kingdom of God. We are called to share with the very poor not in order to humiliate or diminish them but to enable them in turn to be generous, as is normally their inclination.

'Avoid wasteful use of resources and show care for the environment.'

This commitment follows our recognition of the twin evils of pollution and profligacy. It is spelled out in more detail in the first of our Guidelines in which we are called on to 'encourage the renovation, repair, reuse or recycling of materials and products as may be appropriate'. In this as in other matters Life Stylers are swimming against the tide of the market-place. We need all the support from each other that we can get. That is the main reason why our Movement is necessary. Of course to 'show care for the environment' is not merely or even mainly a matter of personal habits (no litter, for example). It at once involves us in political action and leads us naturally on to the next commitment.

'Work with others for social justice through appropriate political action.'

There are Christians who are tempted to oppose personal faith and life to public life and political action. Life Style emphatically repudiates this attitude. If anything the emphasis on 'appropriate political action' has been growing in the Movement over the years and we are pleased to see this development reflected in the life of the worldwide Church as a whole. Even for the comparatively powerless, political action with and for the impoverished and the oppressed is possible at local, national and international level, both as individuals and, more effectively, by mobilising local churches and local councils of churches. Effective work is done by joining and supporting pressure groups such as Amnesty International, the World Development Movement, Shelter and a host of others whose work has a political dimension. Members of Life Style are encouraged to be politically active according to their opportunities in solidarity with the poor and the oppressed.

'Enjoy such good things as are compatible with this commitment.'

This final point in our Commitment distances us from a negative, falsely puritanical attitude to the 'good things' of life. Enjoyment is a key concept of the Life Style Movement. Indeed life is more enjoyable if we learn to live within our incomes, both personally and nationally, and free ourselves from the tyranny of material possessions. The first superficial impression that our emphasis on simple living might give to some enquirers could be of a denial of fullness of life. The exact opposite is the case (as is true of Christian discipline generally), as becomes explicit in this point of our Commitment.

'Share my commitment with others.'

Like the Church the Life Style Movement is committed

to growth. Sharing lies at the heart of it. If material goods are to be shared so are spiritual goods. If we believe that a life of voluntary simplicity is both a duty and a joy, then we are bound to try to share this belief with others. Like many members of the Church, we Life Style members are sometimes diffident about sharing our convictions because we are afraid of being thought to be setting ourselves up as better than others. Such fears, however, should not be indulged. We must have the courage of our convictions.

THE GUIDELINES

Historically these Guidelines derive from the fact that our original Commitment was a fuller, longer document. This original Commitment is set out in *Life Style – A Parable of Sharing*. Over the years it became apparent that a shorter, more concise Commitment would both prove more attractive to the enquirer and retain the essentials. But we were reluctant to lose altogether some of the points in the original Commitment and, indeed, wanted to add to them some further points that had arisen. Hence the Guidelines are intended to complement the Commitment which remains the primary document of the Movement.

The first Guideline reads as follows:

1. Decide what to buy, how much to spend, and what to do without, as befitting those who want fair shares for all; resist the pressures of advertising to buy what in fact you don't need or want; where possible challenge wasteful packaging, built-in obsolescence and bad workmanship; encourage the renovation, repair, reuse or recycling of materials and products as may be appropriate.

This Guideline fills out the Commitment to 'live more simply that all of us may simply live'. The motive for our moderation is our desire for 'fair shares for all'. We are not committed to buying only what we 'need'. What we 'want' is also legitimate provided that our wants are genuine and not extravagant. The words 'where possible' and 'as may be appropriate' recognise that we are not free agents in the matter.

We may wish, for example, to buy 'generic' rather than 'brand-name' drugs; shaving sticks rather than aerosol shaving cream; free range rather than battery-produced eggs. But it is not always possible to fulfil such wishes. Those of us who feel it right to buy a car may want one that is both in the smallest and least powerful class and also will last for twenty years. We may be forced to choose between a larger and a less lasting model. The main point is to make our decisions consciously in the light of principle and not just drift along on the consumerist tide.

2. Decide what percentage of your net disposable income to give away for the benefit of those in need, especially in the developing continents; review this decision regularly and make this amount a first charge on the way you spend the money at your disposal; as an effective sign of this intention, decide whether regularly to do without a meal and gladly give to the hungry the money so saved.

This Guideline fills out the commitment to 'give more freely that others may be free to give'. 'Net disposable income' is capable of various interpretations. To me it would represent the income available after the deduction of rates, taxes and national insurance contributions which are demanded by law, but not mortgage payments or voluntary savings contributions or other regular claims on our incomes which we have voluntarily undertaken. It is not required that we 'regularly do without a meal', only that we decide whether to do so. I did so myself for a time, but somehow got slack about it and haven't continued. Perhaps writing this will enable a fresh start as reading this may similarly enable you. The word 'gladly' in the final

sentence is important. We have it on apostolic authority
that 'God loves a cheerful giver' (II Cor. 9:7).

> 3. Be generous without ostentation and hospitable without
> extravagance; neither eat nor drink to excess, nor consume
> what in your judgment depends for its production on the
> deprivation or exploitation of the poor; make time in your life
> for reflection, for the deepening of your understanding of the
> world in which you live and of the people in it, for recreation
> and for the sharing of simple pleasures with others, and for
> sufficient sleep for good health and good temper [!]; in your
> proper concern for all, do not neglect those near and dear to
> you or any others towards whom you have particular obli-
> gations; in all things enjoy what you have and share it with
> others.

This Guideline fills out the commitments to 'avoid wasteful use of resources and show care for the environment'
and to 'enjoy such good things as are compatible with this
Commitment'. Again the emphasis is on individual judgment and decision. It is not easy to decide what products
depend on the deprivation or exploitation of the poor.
Many, indeed most workers on tea plantations are seriously exploited. But if we ceased to consume their product, so
it is argued, they would be wholly without employment.
Similar considerations apply to a wide range of products,
including sugar, coffee, bananas and many others. Fortu-
nately organisations such as the World Development
Movement and magazines such as the New Internptional-
ist supply us with the materials for an informed judgment
on such questions.

'Reflection' and the 'deepening of understanding' are
essential to an appropriate life style for today and tomorrow. It is not only that we live in a very complex world but
also that unless we reflect and study we shall simply take
the line of least resistance and be swept along with the tide
of consumerism. The recommendations of 'recreation',
'the sharing of simple pleasures' and 'sufficient sleep'

mark our Movement as concerned with personal moderation rather than heroic asceticism, as a Movement to which reasonable women and men might assent. The obligation not to neglect those near and dear to us is of a piece, guarding against a temptation which besets all of us who try to practise a global vision. Finally, it must by now be obvious that both enjoyment and sharing are essential features of an appropriate life style for today and tomorrow.

> 4. If the opportunity arises join a LIFE STYLE 'cell', or with others form a new one to meet regularly for mutual support, study and action; invite a friend to support and advise you from time to time in the working out of this commitment.

Any 'common discipline' depends for its effectiveness on the 'mutual support' of its members. The word 'cell' was chosen as the name for the local unit of such support because of its organic associations. A cell is a sign of life and growth. Like the Church, the Life Style Movement is inevitably and essentially a missionary movement. It must grow or die. To have any effective influence on the redistribution of the Earth's resources it would have to number its members in hundreds of thousands rather than thousands. Moreover, even that membership would have to continue to be but the tip of an iceberg (not a wholly appropriate metaphor) as indeed it is already. For there are probably already a hundred people who accept and even practise our ideas for every one who is committed to our Movement as such.

In many places there is no Life Style cell and there are many members who do not feel competent to form a new one. In those cases we recommend the selection of a friend to act as consultant in what cannot be other than a deeply personal matter.

THE 'TEN REASONS'

In addition to the five-point Commitment and the four-point Guidelines there is another document that has had a profound influence on our Movement. We know it as the 'Ten Reasons', devised by Dr Jorgen Lissner, a Danish Lutheran, who has given us permission to reproduce and use his list of reasons for choosing a simpler life style. Here it is:

TEN REASONS FOR CHOOSING A SIMPLER LIFE STYLE

by Jorgen Lissner

Today's global realities call for many of us to review our life style. Guidelines for a simpler life style cannot be laid down in universal rules; they must be developed by individuals and communities according to their own imagination and situation.

A simpler life style is not a panacea. It may be embarked upon for the wrong reasons, e.g. out of guilt, as a substitute for political action, or in a quest for moral 'purity'. But it can also be meaningful and significant in some or all of the following ways:

1. as an ACT OF FAITH performed for the sake of personal integrity and as an expression of a personal commitment to a more equitable distribution of the world's wealth;
2. as an ACT OF SELF-DEFENCE against the mind-polluting effects of over-consumption;
3. as an ACT OF WITHDRAWAL from the achievement-neurosis of our high-pressure materialistic societies;
4. as an ACT OF SOLIDARITY with the majority of mankind, which has no choice about life style;
5. as an ACT OF SHARING with others what has been given to us, or of returning what was usurped by us through unjust social and economic structures;
6. as an ACT OF CELEBRATION of the riches found in

creativity, spirituality and community with others rather than in mindless materialism;

7. as an ACT OF PROVOCATION by ostentatious under-consumption to arouse curiosity, leading to dialogue with others about affluence, alienation, poverty and social injustice;

8. as an ACT OF ANTICIPATION of the era when the self-confidence and assertiveness of the underprivileged force new power relationships and new patterns of resource allocation upon us;

9. as an ACT OF ADVOCACY of legislated changes in present patterns of production and consumption in the direction of a new international economic order;

10. as an EXERCISE OF PURCHASING POWER to redirect production away from the satisfaction of artificially created wants towards the supply of goods and services that meet genuine social needs.

The adoption of a simpler life style is meaningful and justifiable for any or all of the above reasons *alone*, irrespective of whether it benefits the underprivileged. Demands for 'proof of effectiveness' in helping the poor only bear witness to the myth that 'they the poor' are the problem, and that 'we the rich' have the solution. Yet – if adopted on a large scale a simpler life style will have significant socio-political side-effects both in the rich and in the poor parts of the world. The two most important side-effects are likely to be economic and structural adjustments and the release of new resources and energies for social change.
(*Reproduced with grateful acknowledgments.*)

Dr Lissner's 'act of faith' comes first 'for the sake of personal integrity and as an expression of personal commitment'. His 'commitment' has the same priority as ours, 'to a more equitable distribution of the world's wealth'.

His second reason, 'as an act of self-defence' reinforces our Movement's insistence on the need for mutual support. 'The mind-polluting effects of over-consumption' are powerfully pervasive. There needs to be a positive 'act of withdrawal' from the current 'achievement neurosis' on the part of those who are capable of various forms of achievement. It is no accident that a majority of the members of Life Style could be stereotyped as 'middle class'. This is not only because, as has been said, all revolutions begin with the bourgeoisie, but also because it is largely within the bourgeoisie that it is culturally and economically probable that individuals will make a positive act of withdrawal from achievement and the material rewards which individual achievement can bring.

The fourth of Dr Lissner's reasons, 'an act of solidarity', is prominent in the language and thought of the Life Style Movement. How far our collective practice achieves 'solidarity with the majority of mankind' is another matter. But that is our intention.

'Sharing', too, the key word in Dr Lissner's fifth reason, is prominent in the Life Style idea. The notion of 'returning what was usurped by us through unjust social and economic structures' is less prominent among us, but historically valid and challenging enough. We in Britain more than others ought to be aware of how much our industrial prosperity was built up on the exploitation of the peoples of our former empire and how far the consequences of that exploitation still prevail.

Dr Lissner's sixth reason, 'an act of celebration' also strikes a chord in the hearts of Life Stylers. I have emphasised more than once in this book the note of joy which properly accompanies an appropriate Life Style for today and tomorrow.

The 'act of provocation by ostentatious underconsumption' is more controversial. But the aim of 'arousing curiosity leading to dialogue with others about affluence, alienation, poverty and social injustice' is wholly shared by our Movement. On the whole we find that the very existence of our Movement and the explicit commitment to it of our members is sufficient to achieve this aim without the need of 'ostentatious underconsumption' – a phrase which to me strikes a false note in an otherwise excellent document.

The eighth reason, an act of anticipation of the era when the self-confidence and assertiveness of the underprivileged 'force new power relationships and new patterns of resource allocation upon us' is important. This process has already begun. When the oil-producing nations quadrupled their prices at a stroke so also at a stroke was the membership of our Movement quadrupled. If we are to bear with equanimity the erosion of our privileged economic position (a process of which we can hardly remain unaware) we shall need a truly global view of human welfare such as our Movement tries to offer.

Dr Lissner's ninth reason, 'an act of advocacy of legislated changes in present patterns of production and consumption' corresponds to the emphasis in our Movement on political action in favour of social justice. If we are to advocate such changes with integrity our own life styles have to be in line with the changes we propose.

His final reason, 'as an exercise of purchasing power' hints at the economic analysis briefly offered in Chapter 3 of the present work whereby the consumer, worldwide, is the next great grouping to assert itself by withholding its vital contribution to the pattern of production and consumption. If there are enough of us with sufficiently high motivation we actually can 'redirect production away from the satisfaction of artificially created wants towards the supply of goods and services that meet genuine social needs'. That would constitute the 'proof of effectiveness' which, as Dr Lissner rightly says in his postscript paragraph, cannot be properly demanded at this time. As he says, such demands 'only bear witness to the myth that "they the poor" are the problem, and that "we the rich" have the solution.'

7

LIFE STYLE AND . . .

As an alternative movement Life Style raises a wide range of questions. In an attempt to examine some of these we have been producing a series of leaflets on 'Life Style and . . .' themes as follows: Life Style and the Peace Movement (October 1982); Life Style and Energy Policy (November 1982); Life Style and Economics (March 1983); Life Style and Technology (March 1983); Life Style and the Environment (April 1983); Life Style and Feelings (September 1983); Life Style and World Development (October 1983); Life Style and Health (December 1983); and Life Style and the Proper Future of Work (February 1984). In this chapter I shall be making some comments on these themes with the help of the leaflets (with acknowledgments where due) in the hope of illustrating the current thinking within our movement.

THE PEACE MOVEMENT

Our leaflet, prepared for Life Style by Dr John West, begins with two quotations, taken from the *New Internationalist* as follows:

> The money required to provide adequate food, water, education, health and housing for everyone in the world has been estimated at seventeen billion dollars a year. It is a huge sum

of money – about as much as the world spends on arms every two weeks.'

At least fifty million people around the world are employed in providing military goods and services; almost 20 per cent of the world's engineers and scientists are engaged in military activities; half a million qualified professionals work in military programmes which spend 35 billion dollars a year in search of new weapons technology; there are now more people in military uniform worldwide than there are teachers.

Starting from the conviction of the intimate relationship between world peace and world development, John West claims that Life Style makes its own modest contribution as a movement which:

(a) diminishes envy and mistrust and fosters a co-operative and rewarding life style in our own comparatively rich countries in the developed world, and

(b) affirms the dignity of, and liberates resources for the deprived people of the Third World.

He then distinguishes three broad ways of working for world peace:

1. that we should press for PEACE AT ANY PRICE;

2. that we should accept only PEACE WITH JUSTICE;

3. that we should hope for peace with justice . . . but allow ONLY 'CONVENTIONAL ARMAMENTS'.

These he believes to be the broad alternatives which confront the individual consciences of Life Style members. He then offers the following considerations that should be taken into account as we make our choices:

(a) National and sectional interests are divisive and we should as far as possible adopt a world-scale vision . . .

(b) Ideological differences about the important freedoms . . . are ill served by actions that prove to limit freedom or depress the quality of life . . .

(c) The production of armaments of any kind consumes limited resources of manpower, invention, fossil fuels and metals, and also diverts money into non-productive areas;

(d) . . . mistrust engendered by the possession of arms fuels the arms race;

(e) The chief hope for the human family – and that hope is slim enough – is to restore equity in the use of resources and to improve housing, education, food and health throughout the world.

John adds a short bibliography and a list of the following 'Peace contacts':

The Stockholm International Peace Research Institute (SIPRI)

The Armament and Disarmament Information Unit (ADIU), Sussex University

The School of Peace Studies, Bradford University BD7 1DP

Quaker Peace and Service, London NW1 2BJ

Anglican Pacifist Fellowship, St Mary's Church House, Bayswater Road, Headington, Oxford OX3 9EY

The Peace Tax Campaign. Stanley Keeble, Little Nantesque, Allet, Truro, Cornwall.

Accepting as I do John's assumption that membership of the Life Style Movement does not confine us to any particular solution to the problems attached to our search for world peace, I wish only to add that of his three options I prefer the third, to hope for peace with justice but to abjure the use of nuclear weapons. In particular I cannot see any purpose in my own country's possession of a so-called independent nuclear deterrent and so am committed to its abolition and the banishment of all nuclear weapons from our soil.

I am myself a multilateralist in that I believe that the Soviet Union would be willing to pay a substantial price of disarmament, either nuclear or conventional or both, in return for such an initiative on our part. I do not understand how anyone who claims to be in favour of multilateral disarmament can also be in favour of the deployment of Cruise and Trident missiles in this country. I believe that those who are committed to the Peace Movement should be active in support of practical measures, such as the abolition of these particular weapons, or the establishment of a nuclear freeze, or whatever their personal judgment deems best.

Jesus calls us to be *peacemakers*, i.e. active for peace, not just desirous of it. It is indeed possible for people seriously to believe that international peace is best secured by the increase of the nuclear fire-power of their own country. But those who believe that should not also claim to be in favour of disarmament, multilateral or other. The Life Style Movement, like the gospel, commits us to be active for world peace.

LIFE STYLE AND ENERGY POLICY

This leaflet was also prepared by Dr John West. In it he first lists the main sources of energy – coal, oil, nuclear, electricity (secondary source), solar, hydro, wind, wave and tidal – briefly characterising each one. A correspondent has pointed out the omission of biogas, a singularly appropriate source of energy. Acknowledging his debt to Gerald Foley, *The Energy Question*, John makes the point that the 'energy crisis' is both permanent and world-wide.

Eliminating waste becomes a matter of paramount importance for everyone. The attitude of frugality must be cultivated assiduously in all aspects of consumption . . . Beyond the problem of eliminating waste lies that of adjusting society and its activities, so that an optimum use can be made of whatever energy resources the future may provide. In addition to technical and physical changes, we shall require to re-evaluate our social goals.

In addition to a brief bibliography John West proposes that members of Life Style should ask the following questions about any national or international policy on energy:

1. Does it make thrifty use of the resources we have?
2. Do we need it?
3. Does it promote a fairer share of resources between nations?
4. Does it conserve resources for our grandchildren?
5. Does it improve our quality of life?

Now energy seems to me to be the most convenient way of measuring consumption. Our leaflet quotes from *The Energy Question* the statement that

> the gulf between the subsistence economy and the highly developed one depends almost entirely on the relative availability of usable energy within the two societies. The average American directly and indirectly consumes over 330 times as much fuel-energy as the average Ethiopian.

Clearly, therefore, Life Style's call to 'live more simply that all of us may simply live' is directly relevant to the conservation of energy that is so urgently needed, particularly in the Western world. This is an additional reason why readers of this book should join us. Only if Life Style members increase massively in numbers shall we make any significant impact on energy conservation by our refusal to buy large cars, to overheat our houses; by our encouragement of the use of alternative sources of energy and of research into the appropriate technology for that use; and in our raising of the collective consciousness of *the grave dangers* that attend our current profligacy.

LIFE STYLE AND ECONOMICS

This leaflet was prepared for Life Style by the Rev. Robert Van der Weyer, Hon. Treasurer of the Life Style

Movement and himself a lecturer in economics at the University of Cambridge. He points out that our Movement is 'primarily about a change in economic life'. Such a change has its effect on all the other issues with which we are concerned. Gandhi for example pointed out that peace and non-violence were only possible if economic exploitation ceased and people learned to live simply. Life Style affects economics in two ways: 'as a sign of right economic life, a prophetic witness of a new economic order; and as a practical means of bringing about that new order.'

Robert Van der Weyer finds that

the present economic order, both in its left-wing and its right-wing forms, is based on three moral beliefs:
1. Its view of man: people are seen as fundamentally self-interested, seeking satisfaction in every greater consumption of goods and services. So economic growth is the central goal of policy . . .
2. Its view of relationships: The economic system is seen as based on bargaining and the exercise of power. Under capitalism power depends on the ownership of resources and bargaining takes place in free markets. Under socialism economic power depends on political power and bargaining takes place within central bureaucracies. Either way material success accrues to the powerful, with the weak cast into poverty.
3. Its view of time: over the past two centuries people have come to believe in continual material progress. Our economy depends on unceasing growth to contain the latent conflicts between people.

By contrast the Life Style Movement practises and proclaims a different economic morality as follows:

1. . . . Self-interest is replaced by a desire to co-operate with others, that through common material life we may grow together in spirit; and, as we grow in spiritual solidarity, so material exploitation is replaced by a desire for economic

justice. Simplicity does not mean material deprivation but rather shared prosperity in harmony with the environment.

2. Relationships are seen as based not merely on power but on mutual responsibility; the individual is the steward or trustee of resources for the common good . . .

3. Life Style is a sign of hope for the future . . . Only if we can learn to co-operate and work for the common good shall we be able to stem the increasing material destitution and spiritual despair of our people.

So much for the Life Style Movement as 'a sign of right economic life'. As a practical economic policy,

Life Style offers a way forward by radically altering the agenda of economic policy. It is not in the power of central government to make the changes which are needed . . . It is at the level of small groups that the way forward is to be found . . . Co-operation requires people to live and work in groups where they know each other personally, where economic relationships are also personal relationships. Mutual responsibility requires all those affected by decisions to be involved in making the decisions, not by casting a vote in an impersonal ballot but through listening and responding to one another's attitudes and needs.

Robert ends his statement with this paragraph:

The Life Style Movement is far more revolutionary in its implications than any communist or fascist revolution. But, unlike such revolutions, it is based on love, faith and hope: love for one another; faithful commitment to work for the common good; and hope that out of crisis a new order can emerge.

He also adds four questions for group discussion:

1. Do you agree that Life Style is revolutionary?
2. Do you agree that 'the next step is to become involved in small groups'?

3. Does living more simply increase unemployment?
4. Is Life Style a mere salve for the conscience of the rich?

But the question which I wish to raise is whether there is a convergence between his 'economics as if people mattered', the subtitle of *Small is Beautiful* by the late Dr Schumacher, and my own proposals in Chapter 3 that the consumers of the world should unite to withhold their consumption of what does not advance the common good. I believe that these two ideas do converge, are complementary. The process which I envisage is so revolutionary that it is unlikely to get off the ground, unless by means of small, highly motivated groups. Every ideology has its own 'economics', Marxist, capitalist or whatever. So Life Style implies Schumacher's 'economics as if people mattered'. It seems to imply his 'small is beautiful' as well.

LIFE STYLE AND TECHNOLOGY

This leaflet has also been written for Life Style by Dr John West. I am glad that he devotes a substantial proportion of the space available to a repudiation of the notion that Life Style is opposed to technology. He writes:

What is often forgotten is that the fruits of technology . . . include pharmaceuticals (analgesics, anaesthetics, antidepressants, vaccines and antibiotics); mains water, sewage and drainage; domestic heating, lighting and insulation; comfortable and safe public transport systems; refrigerated food storage and preservation techniques; modern reproduction and printing techniques, books, newspapers, files, records, the telephone, ballpoint pens, tools, spectacles, adhesives; to say nothing of the manufacture of our basic raw materials such as metals, glass, bricks, cement, rubber, plastics and paper. In short, 'TECHNOLOGY' EMBRACES MANUFACTURING TECHNIQUES OF ALL KINDS, most of which have advanced as a result of the discoveries and applications of science . . . So, technology puts the water in your tap, provides the instruments for the *Brandenburg Concerto* and the typewriter on which this was written. Much, then, as some of us may regret the passing of the idyllic pastoral life (often viewed through unrealistically rosy spectacles!) the majority of us live in cities and we would all regret the absence of aspirin, sanitary towels, modern hard-wearing shoes and socks, comfortable houses, fast inter-city transport – and, indeed, of bicycles.

Doth he protest too much? I would not have quoted this paragraph at length if I had thought so. For, as I speak about the Life Style Movement up and down the country, I often get the impression that at least some of the audience expect our Movement to fall within the category of a romantic attempt to set the clock back. But there is of course what John calls 'a grey area' of technological products, among which he includes:

the contraceptive pill, the private car, the deep freezer, television, the automatic washing machine, computerised systems for storing and displaying information, tranquillisers, digital watches, throw-away nappies, plastic tableware, and many others.

Most of the items on this list I would myself find acceptable, but I welcome the following questions which John supplies as criteria:

1. Does it contribute to the goal of co-existence of all human beings in peace, human dignity and self-fulfilment?
2. Does it minimise danger, noise, strain or the invasion of privacy?
3. Does it minimise pollution, promote the beauty of our environment and help wild life?
4. Does it contribute to our stewardship of mineral and energy resources?

I must say that these seem rather grand questions to ask about such artefacts as throw-away nappies or plastic tableware, as does the final question which John borrows with acknowledgment from Professor Thring: 'Can it be available to all the eight to ten billion people who will be in the world in the next century?' Let us not take ourselves too seriously. So I am glad that John ends his paper by saying: 'If it has a high FUN value, making our life more convenient and those around you more happy, that too may constitute a good reason for your choice. The choice is your own and the guidelines mine!'

After the brief bibliography that is customary in these leaflets he goes on to pose these questions for group discussion:

1. Do you agree with the criteria proposed for assessing the acceptability of any technological innovation? In particular, is the 'key question' about availability to all too stringent? What other criteria would you adopt?
2. Is fun or recreational advantage a sufficient excuse for indulgence? Do you agree with those who argue that we should all accept a lower level of comfort (lower house temperature in winter, no fridge or freezer, no car) and that Life Style requires us to enjoy austerity?
3. Should individual households aim for self-sufficiency? Is this aim possible for city dwellers?'

I leave the reader to answer these questions for her or himself, only observing that the Life Style Movement contains within its adherents a wide variety of answers.

LIFE STYLE AND THE ENVIRONMENT

There is a small group of Christians who, at the time of writing, are setting up their own separate life style movement on the grounds that we are 'too ecological'. I cannot myself understand how Christians can become 'too ecological' since our doctrines of the creation of the world and its cosmic redemption would seem to commit us to a deep and loving care for it. So we have a leaflet on 'Life Style and the Environment' prepared for us by John West and Clare Enright. In the introductory sheet for the whole series of these leaflets the paragraph on the environment leaflet reads:

> Modern farming methods mostly use high energy inputs, displace labour, de-condition the soil and pollute water sources. As such they are inappropriate for use in tropical countries. We must preserve the wilderness areas as reservoirs for wildlife and for our own refreshment.

The leaflet roots our concern for the whole environment firmly in what has to be thought of as our overriding concern for world development, for the fulfilment of the basic needs of the human family.

> Our concern for the living world becomes most urgent when we consider the rapid increase in human population in the developing countries and their need for sufficient and appropriate food . . . This pamphlet therefore deals with food production, pollution and the conservation of natural resources.

The leaflet's main section, under the heading of 'Food Production', begins with the statement that 'the first call on land use must be to feed the world's growing population'. There follows a well-argued plea for appropriate agricultural technology, less energy- and capital-intensive. This section ends with the following particular illustration which establishes the link between our personal life styles and the whole environmental issue.

> In the UK we have become accustomed to a meat diet. And yet meat production, particularly at an intensive level, is a wasteful process in terms of land and energy and it consumes

grain that is sorely needed by the malnourished millions in the Third World. For this reason, many Life Stylers have severely limited their meat intake or become vegetarian. The wider adoption of plant produce as our main source of protein would do much to alleviate the problems of world food production.

The second and last section of this leaflet is headed 'Non-agricultural lands' and contains a plea for the retention of 'refuge areas' in 'recognition of the interdependence of everything in the biosphere'. A further important point is made in the last paragraph:

Areas of natural vegetation serve a further important purpose. The vast majority of animal and plant species exist only in the wild and these areas form a reservoir of genetic material. This enables them to respond to environmental changes.

After the usual brief bibliography, Clare and John submit the following questions for group discussion:

Do you agree that we are stewards or should we use the earth's resources for humanity's benefit only? Is population control the major priority? Can one divorce land use from the issue of ownership?

I would agree that as human beings we are God's stewards with a responsibility for the whole of his creation, both animate and inanimate, but that we have a higher level of responsibility towards our fellow human beings. Often these responsibilities cohere. For example, it is in the interests both of the human population and of the whole natural habitat that we stop destroying the Himalayan forests and the Amazonian jungles. Sometimes they are, in the short term at least, opposed. The interests of the Bengal tiger may be opposed to those of the poverty-stricken tribal peoples who share the tiger's habitat. Some balance has to be maintained.

Is population control the major priority? The population explosion comes under control only when extreme poverty is diminished. For it is extreme poverty that leads to the economic necessity of bringing into the world large families. In general therefore the major priority is the control, leading to the abolition of extreme poverty.

Can one divorce land use from the issue of ownership? I am glad that Clare and John raise this question because I believe, in general, that if you consult the very poor, you find that land ownership is for many of them a very basic issue. Borrowing money on the security of your land in a bad year or to pay for a wedding has been for many the first step on the slippery slope towards destitution. Ownership of enough land for subsistence farming gives a family a basic security. The landless are the exploited ones in an economy where there is massive unemployment. As with the enclosure movement in eighteenth-century Britain, the introduction of improved methods of agricultural production today, the so-called 'green revolution', often enables the rich to prosper and to dispossess the poor of what land they have. In Kerala in South-West India some years ago many Christians, who form a sizeable minority in that state, gave their support to a communist state government, largely because of the land reforms which they promised to introduce.

LIFE STYLE AND FEELINGS

As its title suggests this leaflet deals with a private rather than a public concern. 'Prepared for Life Style by Dilys and John West, with a little help from their friends,' it 'airs difficult feelings about living more simply in a consumerist society, and discusses ways of coping with guilt and anger'. As such it could prove to be the most important in the series. Other leaflets deal with great issues, inevitably in a generalised way because of their brevity.

But this one deals with the profound feelings of personal joy and personal alienation, personal guilt and personal liberation, experienced by those who swim against the great tide of consumerism.

The first part of this leaflet (under the heading 'Sharing the shadow' (Dilys West)) gives a personal account of the anger experienced in facing 'the demands that my commitment makes on me'. 'Trying to live simply is one of the hardest things I have ever done.'

> Shortly we shall be moving from a home I love, on which I've spent much physical and emotional energy, to a smaller, less convenient house. If all goes well this move will not only enrich our lives but also release some of our resources; hopefully we shall be living more simply so that perhaps one other person may simply live. Yet I feel a great sadness and not a little anger at the prospect. I hope out of this sadness and anger will come the joy of living more simply, with less space and fewer possessions. I am not proud of these feelings. I know I'm lucky to have a home, enough to eat and other blessings. But I need to share these feelings. It is also my hope that sharing them in this way may help others, especially those wondering whether they should take the plunge and commit themselves to Life Style.

This section of the leaflet ends with an invitation to join us. 'So to anyone out there who might happen to read this: join us.' And with a well-known quotation from Edmund Burke: 'For evil to triumph it is only necessary for good men and women to do nothing.'

The second part of the leaflet is headed 'Dealing constructively with anger'. The authors suggest that

> We must first UNDERSTAND our anger's true origin, bearing in mind that we are very good at hiding unpleasant truths from ourselves. (For example, anger may arise from feelings of insecurity or lack of an acceptable identity, yet we 'project' our anger by blaming someone else.) . . . Another

view is that, if we feel a strong emotion, we should EXPRESS it at the time . . . but we have to beware of hurting anyone who is vulnerable. The problem we face in acting out our anger is the guilt we feel or the damage we do.

Such selective quotation can never do justice to what is presented to us as a coherent whole. The leaflet ends by proposing that 'the most constructive way of using your anger is to let it drive you into FIGHTING INJUSTICE, opposing waste and lobbying for the underprivileged. Angry people are best able to step out of line. Angry can be good.'

The following 'questions for discussion' are appended:

1. Since joining Life Style, what do you no longer
   (a) buy?
   (b) do?
   Which of these decisions makes you feel most liberated and which do you miss most? Do any of them make you feel angry or resentful, either occasionally or all the time?
2. If you occasionally feel angry or deprived by the self-imposed demands of Life Style, how do you react: Count your blessings? Discuss with a friend? Go out on a binge? Any other suggestions? Should you revise or revoke that particular Life Style decision?
3. Which of the following would you be prepared to share with:
   (a) someone you know would treat it carefully?
   (b) just anyone?
   Lawnmower, bicycle, freezer, vacuum cleaner, sewing machine, record player/music centre, musical instrument, typewriter, microcomputer, car, home . . . (please add to the list).
4. Does the possession of any of the above by a Life Styler shock you? If you possess some or all of them, do you feel guilty about doing so?

Once again I leave the sympathetic reader to apply these questions to his or her own Life Style. My own comment

concerns the more positive feelings engendered by trying
to live more simply so that all of us may simply live.

It is no fault of the leaflet that it deals mainly with the
negative feelings. For that is its purpose. However one of
the most negative feelings that we may experience when
we contemplate the gross injustice in the world is a feeling
of importance. What on earth can I do? Life Style asserts
your personal significance and persuades you that you can
do something. Your own life style is at least partially under
your control. Begin from there. Many Life Style members
have discovered in their membership a feeling of liberation from a sense of complete helplessness.

Guilt is a more complex feeling to handle than helplessness. Collectively most of those who read this book are the
aggressors, those who benefit substantially from the injustice in the world. Feelings of guilt are often experienced as
we come to know the real facts, the structural connection
between the wealth of the West and the poverty of others.
But it is my experience and that of others that such feelings
are considerably assuaged by joining in a Commitment
which marks you out as in favour of a more equitable
distribution of the Earth's resources and helps to bring
your life style into line.

So the assuaging of feelings of helplessness and guilt
does lead to a sense of well-being (not complacency, I
hope) and a real joy. Life is also much more comfortable
and relaxed when liberated from the urge to make more
and more money in order to consume more and more
goods and services.

For the Christian all this is in the context of his or her
faith, the assurance of God's forgiveness and the desire to
be obedient to God's will. The sense of being in a small
way a pioneer, of being committed to an idea whose time
has come is immensely enhanced by a belief that such a
commitment is also a contribution to the kingdom of God.
Joining the Life Style Movement may cause a degree of
alienation, the mockery of some of your friends, in some

cases conflict even within your family. But it also wins you new friends, including some very lovely people. As I write of the feelings of being a member of Life Style, I am struck by how similar they are to those of being committed to the Christian faith.

LIFE STYLE AND WORLD DEVELOPMENT

The reader may be surprised that this subject comes only seventh in our series of leaflets. The order was somewhat conditioned by the order of subjects for recent Life Style weekend conferences. We tend to produce a leaflet as a result of a conference.

In the leaflet which introduces the series we read about this one that

World trade has had mostly harmful effects on the poorer countries and official 'aid' continues to exploit them. We must work for their self-reliance and be ourselves prepared to learn community values and thrift from those apparently worse off. It is not a matter of how much we give but of how much we are prepared to stop taking.

As an economist and a Christian, Robert Van der Weyer, who prepared this leaflet for us, is acutely aware of the injustice of the present situation. 'Our attitudes and policies,' he writes in his introductory paragraph, 'for world development are littered with shortsighted self-interest and misguided altruism.'

Under the heading 'Trade and Development' he criticises the nineteenth-century notion that free trade would be 'the main engine for development. Economists have taught that if each country specialises in those products to which it is best suited, and trades freely with other countries, then all shall be richer.'

Sadly the results have been different. 'India for example, had been one of the richest countries in the world; but, as Gandhi never tired of explaining, trade with the West had ruined its staple industries of spinning and weaving, which in turn had undermined its entire rural economy.'

In the twentieth century a similar fate is overtaking the Western world. 'The rapid collapse of manufacturing industry in the West is reflected in the rapid rise of new industries in the East, under-pricing Western products and causing widespread and growing unemployment.'

Under the heading 'Aid and Development' Robert makes a similar judgment about aid. He points out that countries such as Tanzania and Bangladesh which have received massive amounts of aid remain very poor, whereas such countries as Taiwan and South Korea have prospered with the help of commercial private investment. He adds:

> There is, however, a deeper objection to much of what passes for aid. We are rightly critical of the nineteenth-century missionaries who, in seeking to propagate the Christian gospel, also exported Western secular values, in the conviction that western culture was intrinsically superior. The belief that the development of Asia and Africa should involve investment and economic growth along a similar line to that of the West is based on the same cultural paternalism. Sadly the West has been far more successful in exporting its religion of economic growth than in proclaiming the gospel of the poor man from Nazareth.

These radical objections to much current world trade and development aid were discussed at a Life Style weekend conference. They proved too much for many members to stomach, accustomed as we were to a more positive attitude both to freedom of trade and to 'real aid' as it is currently being defined by governments and development agencies. There was much more support, however, for the very positive role which Robert found for Life Style in his scenario. His third and last section, entitled 'Life Style and Development', sketches out this role.

The Life Style movement is one element in a widespread questioning and reappraisal of western economic and social values. The belief that continued economic growth and an ever-rising standard of living is the path to human fulfilment is now discredited . . . world development can no longer be seen as a question of the West helping the poorer countries to 'catch up', but rather as a search for social values and economic structures which can offer a fulfilling and sustaining way of life. The Life Style motto is a signpost in this search. Our first task is remedial, to try to eliminate the exploitative trading relationships on which our luxurious way of life is based . . .

The values on which world development should be based involve a renewal of the local economic community, in which work is not merely a way of gaining money but is perceived as a service to the group to which the individual belongs. Gandhi is the great prophet of our century who saw this clearly: he realised that the so-called 'under-developed' economies of Asia and Africa were far better placed than the industrial economies of the West. This means that the most important exchange between one country and another is not of goods but of EDUCATION: we have much to learn from Asia and Africa, as they may still do from us.

Robert ends with a paragraph which challenges the individual reader and places the Life Style Movement firmly in the van of economic change:

For each individual the starting point of a commitment to world development of this kind is a change of life style from affluence to simplicity, from individualism to community involvement. This should not be based on some misplaced altruism but rather on a desire for self-education, so that we may begin to learn for ourselves the way in which the human family must develop in the years ahead.

As I have already hinted, this leaflet 'represents a personal view, and not necessarily that of the Life Style Movement'. But my guess is that an increasing number of Life Style members will come round to something like the critical view of trade and aid, as they are at present practised, and the centrality which Robert gives to the need for fundamental changes in values and therefore in life styles in the West. The 'real aid' movement being promoted within the development agencies is in the right direction. Many Christians and others who are concerned with world development will continue to hold an ambivalent view of free trade. On the one hand, we shall see the force of Robert's strictures upon it. On the other we shall be most reluctant to see any increase in the already considerable restrictions which the more powerful nations impose on the exports of the less powerful in order to protect their own industries. There must be many instances in which freedom of trade would benefit the less affluent and the less profligate.

The leaflet concludes with three questions:

1. Should we try to buy goods from the poorer countries, e.g. via Bridge and Traidcraft? Does such aid encourage the wrong sort of development, over-reliant on Western money and markets, or does it encourage self-sufficiency?
2. Should we give money to charity organisations, or is such aid ineffective in reaching the truly poor? Should we distinguish between gifts for disaster relief and gifts for long-term development projects, and, if so, why? How can we hope to influence the social and structural factors which cause poverty?
3. How might changes in our personal life style influence the kinds of development in the poorer countries? What can we learn about life style from the poorer countries?

LIFE STYLE AND HEALTH

In this paper John West says that there is no specifically Life Style view on health, but that Life Style does presuppose a particular perspective on medical services, their use and abuse, both at home and abroad. Our concern for a more equitable distribution of the Earth's resources leads us to an emphasis on primary health care. In poorer countries this must mean the provision of 'sufficient affordable food, clean water and basic sanitation – allied of course to health education, family planning and immunisation'. In the UK we need 'wider community health care and the removal of poverty and the stress of unemployment'.

Under the heading of 'Appropriate medicine' John goes on to complain that in the West

> the romantic appeal of cancer research and heart transplants is akin to the 'Concorde Syndrome' that has distorted so much of our science and engineering . . . At the same time countless women endure painful periods and menopauses; countless men have to wait for hernia and prostate operations; most of the mentally ill have to endure needless pain and inadequate counselling; many others suffer minor but crippling complaints that the social and medical services are not equipped to meet.

The final section in this leaflet is entitled 'State versus private versus alternative medicine'. The writer believes that the use of 'private medicine' is 'permissible' to Life Stylers 'to reduce waiting times or to obtain more leisured and personal treatment' provided that 'the wider adoption of private medicine' does not 'remove essential staff or funding from the basic NHS needs'. He concludes with a short plea on behalf of

> an alternative style of medicine. The practitioners of such alternatives as homeopathy and acupuncture argue that they

treat the whole person rather than presenting symptoms . . .
Alternative medicine tends to use 'low technology', relatively
cheap apparatus and procedures whose wider adoption could
save resources. But this is not an either-or debate.

Like others in the series this leaflet concentrates on the
'public' aspects of the issue. Had I been writing it I should
have tried to bring out the positive effects of a deliberately
simpler life style on personal health. Less meat, less
alcohol, no smoking; less eating and drinking generally;
more walking instead of driving a car; fewer overheated
rooms; less anxiety about money and possessions; with a
consequent diminution of overwork. All these are generally beneficial to the health of those who have such
choices. There is, I believe, a direct connection between
the adoption of a simpler life style and good health. Many
members of Life Style would eschew private medicine on
the grounds that it does compete with the NHS. Others
might not give such prominence to 'alternative medicine'
in so short an article. However, as John makes clear, these
are matters of personal opinion. He appends the following
questions for discussion:

1. Do you agree that there are primarily social causes for ill
   health? Does this mean that Life Stylers should work
   politically for favourable changes in these background
   factors rather than for body-scanners and other technological advances?
2. Do you consider that 'alternative' medicine is more
   person-centred than conventional medicine and so more
   appropriate to living simply?
3. Do you approve of private medical services? Should expen-
   sive techniques be restricted to the private sector?

LIFE STYLE AND THE PROPER FUTURE OF WORK

This, the final leaflet to be produced up to the end of 1984, is specifically based on the discussions at a weekend conference at Whalley Abbey. An introductory paragraph ends with the statement that

> we now see that, in a finite world, competition is destructive: pollution, resource depletion and unemployment are symptoms of a moral sickness. What makes unemployment possible is a world view that encompasses privilege and subordination, that places value on what an article costs rather than its usefulness, and that sees money as an end and human beings as a means to that end.

Under the heading 'Appropriate Work' we read that

> a transformation is needed . . . we must devise financial structures that give people opportunities to develop their faculties and co-operate in a common task of meeting their own and others' real needs. This also means giving far more weight to the 'informal economy' of unpaid work in the home and in the community, including parenting and caring, and also recognising the vital place of recreation in being a whole person. It also means establishing a world economic system that can gear global production of goods and services to the real needs of the whole human family.

I should myself wish to emphasise this last point. The Life Style Movement's concern for 'a more equitable distribution of the Earth's resources among the whole human family' seems to me to converge on the need to reduce massively the levels of unemployment throughout the world. Up to a thousand million people live in degrading poverty today. To fulfil their basic needs indefinitely would provide employment for millions. But at present the only people who could pay for such a fulfilment are the rich. Only if the rich voluntarily surrender part of their inordinate claims can such a transformation take place. Life Style is about such a voluntary surrender. The leaflet continues:

> For such a transformation to be possible we must move from consumerism and the production of useless or wasteful goods (especially armaments!) to a system that involves close international co-operation and the recognition of our interdependence in a finite eco-sphere. At the practical level we must lobby for such a structural change, promote the development of co-operatives, encourage intervention by government to achieve a more equitable distribution of work and income, question the value systems of the community and their expectations about adult life, question the market economy and the economic systems of ownership and power ('The protestant work ethic was the ethic of those who had the power to organise work' – Blum), and question ideas about efficiency and cost. At the same time, the Life Style Movement can demonstrate that the quality of life does not rest upon how much we consume, that co-operation and sharing are possible at many levels, that people's value lies in their personal qualities rather than in terms of what they do.

Under the heading 'Alleviating the Pain' the leaflet goes on to suggest five spheres of immediate action: through MPs and political parties; through trades union membership; through management; through local councils; through voluntary agencies. After the usual short bibliography it concludes with five 'questions for group discussion':

1. Should Life Style members act politically?
2. Is short-term expediency (reducing inflation) an acceptable reason for making unemployment worse? Are 'market forces' sufficiently flexible, visionary, or people-centred, or should economists adopt the 'Buddhist economics' advocated by Schumacher and in this Paper?

3. Do you agree that a radical transformation is needed in our approach to work and the fairer distribution of goods and services? How do you see such a transformation being brought about?

4. Is advertising, especially on TV, encouraging too much envy and greed, as well as performing its primary function of informing?

5. Can you suggest other things to do to 'alleviate the pain'?

Questions are occasionally begged by the form in which they are put. It is hardly fair to characterise 'reducing inflation' as a matter of 'short-term expediency'. It is the poor and disadvantaged who are hardest hit by inflation. Life Style members should, I believe, support its control and hope for its elimination. But inflation and high unemployment are not necessary alternatives in a sane economy. A voluntary simplicity of life style makes fewer demands on the economy and would therefore tend to reduce inflation without the consequence of massive unemployment. Indeed, as I have already indicated, a global concentration on fulfilling the basic needs of the whole human family would produce opportunities of employment for all who need them.

I should like to repeat my acknowledgments to John West, who wrote also this last leaflet, and to Clare Enright, Robert Van der Weyer and Dilys West who, as already indicated, co-operated in the writing of other leaflets of this series. In this final chapter there has been less explicit reference to the Christian faith than in other chapters. But I hope that the Christian reader has found nothing in it contrary to that faith and much, indeed, that is congruous to it. As has been said before the Life Style Movement is open to women and men of any faith or none. For its concerns are the concerns of the whole human family. In practice however a majority of its members appear to have been motivated in their membership by the Christian faith, as I have been myself.

LIFE STYLE AND YOU

There is no leaflet with this heading. It is my way of bringing this book to a close. I have sought to establish the following truths on which Christians should act together:

First, Christians are committed by the love of God to work and to pray for 'a more equitable distribution of the Earth's resources and the conservation and development of those resources for our own and future generations'.

Second, this commitment means for those of us who have the choice a life style of voluntary simplicity. We are not to consume an inordinate share of the Earth's resources.

Third, this commitment also steers us towards political action in solidarity with the poor and the oppressed.

Fourth, this commitment is not, however, exclusive to Christians. We Christians should co-operate with others in a commitment which is a sign of being fully human.

Fifth, our commitment runs counter to very powerful forces in contemporary society, whether capitalist or socialist. Increased consumption is generally believed to be conducive to the general good. To challenge this assumption is to swim against a powerful tide of vested interests. We therefore need all the mutual support we can get.

The Life Style Movement is designed to offer that mutual support and so decisively promote an idea whose time has come.

If after reading this book you want either to know even more about the Life Style Movement and receive its literature or (better still) if you want to join us without further ado, write to our general secretary, Mrs Margaret Smith, Manor Farm, Little Gidding, Cambs PE17 5RJ. She will also refer you to your regional and county co-ordinator who can inform you of any Life Style members, cells or activities in your neighbourhood. At the time of writing we have about a thousand members but no paid staff.

BIBLIOGRAPHY

A GENERAL LIST

(Alphabetical order of authors)

NOTE: This general list is based on 'Aids to Life Style: A Short List of Books and Periodicals' compiled by John West with acknowledged 'major help' from Jim and Pauline Bryant, and from Anuradha Vittachi. Reference is also made to the 'valuable portfolio of documents' on alternative life styles issues by the Commission on the Churches' Participation in Development, World Council of Churches, obtainable from 150 Route de Ferney, 1211 Geneva 20, Switzerland.

J. Barr (ed.), *The Environmental Handbook* (Ballantine/FOE). An action guide for the consumer.

Lester Brown, *The Twenty-ninth day: Accommodating Human Needs and Numbers to the Earth's Resources* (Norton). A major contribution to bridging the gap between ecologists and economists.

Lester Brown, Christopher Flavin, Colin Norman, *Running on Empty. The Future of the Automobile in an Oil Short World* (Norton). A Worldwatch Institute book.

David Clark, *Basic Communities. Towards an Alternative Society* (SPCK). A vital handbook of Christian community life in Britain. And more.

David Clark, *The Liberation of the Church* (NACCAN).
Argues the vital role of basic communities in such a liberation.

Erik Dammann, *The Future in Our Hands* (Pergamon Press).
Heartfelt and inspiring, easy to follow. English translation of the
    book which inspired the movement of the same name.

A. H. Dammers, *Life Style – a Parable of Sharing* (Turnstone
    Press).

R. F. Dasmann, *The Conservation Alternative* (Wiley).
A clear statement of ecological principles.

Nigel Dower, *World Poverty. Challenge and Response* (Sessions,
    1983).

David L. Edwards, *The British Churches Turn to the Future*,
    (SCM).
The official account of the Church Leaders' Conference in 1972
    when the Life Style Movement began.

P. Ehrlich, *The Population Bomb* (Ballantine/FOE).
By a leading authority on the population explosion.

Ehrlich and Harriman, *How to be a Survivor* (Pan Books)
A plan to save Spaceship Earth.

Charles Elliott (Chairman), *Real Aid: A Strategy for Britain*
    (Published by the Independent Group on British Aid,
    whose first Report it is).
Essential reading for those concerned with World Development
    issues.

Charles Elliott (Chairman), *Aid is not Enough. Britain and the
    World's Poor*.
Supplements *Real Aid: A Strategy for Britain*. Equally im-
    pressive.

Susan George, *How the Other Half Dies* (Pelican).
Well-researched and convincing claim to present the real reasons
    for the world's hunger.

Tony Gibson, *People Power* (Pelican).
Handbook for those wishing to organise grassroots pressure
　　groups. Includes a 151-page Fact Bank. Sympathetically
　　written.

J. Holliman, *Consumer's Guide to the Protection of the En-
　　vironment*.
Full of practical ideas. Some of the statistics now out of date.

Charles Kiely, *Solar Energy. Do-it-yourself Manual* (Hamlyn).
Practical and detailed.

P. Lavins, *Soft Energy Path* (Ballinger).
Critique of current energy policies.

R. Mabey, *The Pollution Handbook* (Penguin).
Based on a project for children, but enjoyable by all ages.

J. Mallinson, *Christian Life Style* (Obtainable from Renewal
　　Publications, Box 130, West Ryde, 2114 NSW Australia).
Full of ideas for small groups, such as Life Style Cells.

Barbara Maude, *The Turning Tide* (Faber & Faber).
Preparing for the post-surplus society.

W. G. McClelland, *And a New Earth* (Friends' Home Service).
A Quaker's view of how to improve society.

Dianna Melrose, *The Great Health Robbery* (Oxfam).
Baby milk and medicines in the Yemen.

Dianna Melrose, *Bitter Pills* (Oxfam).
The scandal of inappropriate drug marketing and sales in
　　developing countries.

Hugh Montefiore, *Doom or Deliverance* (Manchester University
　　Press).
The Rutherford Lecture for 1971 on the dogmas and duties of a
　　technological age.

Julius Nyerere, *Essays in Socialism* (OUP).
Lucid, basic, unpretentious, warm, persuasive. Not only for
    socialists.

Vance Packard, *The Waste Makers* (Penguin).
Pioneering, readable attack on built-in obsolescence.

Edward Patey, *Christian Life Style* (Mowbrays).
Comprehensive in a short compass, including the political
    dimension.

R. M. Pirsig, *Zen and the Art of Motorcycle Maintenance* (Corgi:
    Bodley Head).
Unusual and very stimulating. Doesn't quite match up to the
    claims on its jacket.

Patrick Rivers, *Living Better on Less* (Turnstone Press).
Life Style in practice.

Patrick Rivers, *The Survivalists* (Universe Books).
Stories of Life Style in practice.

Patrick and Shirley Rivers, *Diet for a Small Island*.
Includes 160 recipes, prefaced by a rationale for eating fresh
    wholefoods.

William Ryan, *Blaming the Victim* (Random House).
Invigorating polemic on how literal do-gooders have it both ways
    at the expense of the poor.

David Sheppard, *Built as a City* (Hodder & Stoughton).
Excellent on God and the urban world today. Reinforces the
    necessity of solidarity with the poor.

David Sheppard, *Bias to the Poor* (Hodder & Stoughton).
Another excellent plea for Christian solidarity with the poor.
    Enriched by the author's considerable urban experience.

Ronald J. Sider, *Rich Christians in an Age of Hunger* (Hodder &
    Stoughton).
Well-documented, biblically based, incontrovertible.

Ronald J. Sider, *Living More Simply* (Hodder & Stoughton).
Case studies from USA of Christians who have practised the
simple living that they preach.

Ronald J. Sider (ed.), *Lifestyle in the Eighties* (Paternoster Press).
Testimonies from a conference on the evangelical commitment
to a simple life style.

Ronald J. Sider (ed.), *Evangelicals and Development* (Paternoster
Press).
The fruit of another consultation. Towards a theology of social
change.

John V. Taylor, *Enough is Enough* (SCM Press).
A pioneering Christian work on our theme. Excellent biblical
section.

Alvin Toffler, *Future Shock* (Pan Books).
Disturbing and challenging on how to deal with rapid change.

Alvin Toffler, *The Third Wave* (Bantam Books).
Brilliant futurology, basically hopeful.

J. Wynne Tyson, *The Civilised Alternative* (Centaur Press).
A pattern for protest.

G. Vickers, *Freedom in a Rocking Boat* (Penguin).
Original discussion of changing values.

B. Ward and R. Dubos, *Only One Earth* (Penguin).
Clear and passionate report for the 1972 UN Conference in
Stockholm. Good summary of our global predicament.

Folkert Wilken, *The Liberation of Capital*.
Radical economics and original ideas.

B ADDITIONAL GENERAL LIST

Willy Brandt (Chairman), *North-South: A Programme for
Survival* (Pan Books).
The first report of the Independent Commission on Inter-
national Development Issues.

Willy Brandt (Chairman), *Common Crisis*.
The second report of the 'Brandt Commission'.

Klaus Bockmuhl, *Conservation and Lifestyle* (Grove Books).
A Grove booklet on ethics with an evangelical background.

Paulo Freire, *Pedagogy of the Oppressed* (Penguin).
Important analysis of some of the blocks to liberation. Difficult,
    condensed style.

Erich Fromm, *To Have or to Be?* (Abacus).
Some basic philosophy.

Paul Harrison, *Inside the Third World*. Also *The Third World
    Tomorrow* (Pelican).
Summary of some problems with proposals for solving them.

Ronald Higgins, *The Seventh Enemy*, (Hodder & Stoughton).
Very similar analysis to that behind the Life Style Movement.
    The 'seventh enemy' is apathy. Life Style members should
    read it.

Eloise Lester(ed.), *Ecology and Christian Responsibility* (Papers
    read at a conference at Sewanee, Tennessee, organised by
    the Community of the Cross of Nails).

D. H. Meadows, D. L. Meadows, J. Randers, W. W. Behrens,
    The Limits to Growth (Earth Island).
Thought-provoking, controversial discussion of resource
    depletion.

Owen Nankivell, *All Good Gifts* (Epworth Press).
A Christian appraisal of global stewardship.

James Robertson, *The Sane Alternative*.
Again the analysis is congenial to the Life Style Movement.
    Balanced and radical.

Mark Satin, *New Age Politics* (Whitecap Books, Vancouver).
Contains a good chapter on voluntary simplicity.

E. F. Schumacher, *Small is Beautiful* (Abacus Press).
'A study of economics as if people mattered'. A classic in this
   field.

E. F. Schumacher, *The Age of Plenty* (St Andrew Press,
   Edinburgh).
Short but penetrating Christian view of the future.

Meredith Thring, *The Engineer's Conscience* (Northgate).
Profound and radical.

C *SOME PERIODICALS*

Good Earth, six issues annually. A newspaper which highlights
   the hazards of current life styles. From 18 Cofton Lane Rd,
   Birmingham B4E 8PL.

Spur News, bulletin which acts as information exchange on
   inequitable trade issues. From 17 Anson Rd, London N7
   ORB.

Conservation News, quarterly journal of the Conservation
   Society. From 12 London St, Chertsey, Surrey KT16 8AA.

New Internationalist, radical, readable, illustrated monthly on
   world development. From 62 High St, Wallingford, Berks.

D *'LIFE STYLE AND . . .' LIST*

(Books not in the General lists above)

I Life Style and the Peace Movement

J. Cox, *Overkill* (Penguin).
Useful on nuclear disarmament.

Freeman Dyson, *Weapons and Hope*, (Harper and Row).
Expert, unusual, hopeful.

N. Humphrey & R. J. Lifton, *In a Dark Time*.
Anti-war anthology. Imaginative and moving selection.

A. Mack & A. Boserup *War without weapons* (Pinter).

E. P. Thompson & Dan Smith, *Protest and Survive* (Penguin).
Essays on Britain's nuclear stance, with special reference to
  Cruise.

The Roman Catholic Bishops (USA), *The Challenge of Peace:
  God's Promise and our Response* (CTS/SPCK).
Pastoral Letter on War and Peace in the Nuclear Age. Carefully
  thought out and authoritative theology.

Working party, Board of Social Responsibility, Church of
  England, *The Church and the Bomb* (Hodder & Stoughton).
After careful and responsible research, the working party,
  chaired by the Bishop of Salisbury, advocates unilateral
  nuclear disarmament for Britain.

Peace News.
Published fortnightly, 30p, from 8 Elm Ave, Nottingham 3.

Sanity.
Published bimonthly at 40p by CND, 11 Goodwin St, London
  N4 3HQ.

Gwyn Prins (ed.), *Defended to Death* (Penguin).

II Life Style and Energy Policy

G. Foley, *The Energy Question* (Penguin).
Our leaflet is indebted to this survey.

G. Leach & others, *A Low Energy Strategy for the United
  Kingdom*.
International Institute for the Environment and Development
  Practical proposals.

III Life Style and Economics

E. F. Schumacher, *Good Work* (Abacus).
Everything he writes is worth reading.

IV Life Style and Technology

M. Cooley, *Architect or Bee?*
Langley Technical Services.

D. Morley, *The Sensitive Scientist* (SCM Press).

V Life Style and the Environment

J. Lenihan & W. W. Fletcher (ed.), *Food, Agriculture and the
    Environment*.

Council on Environmental Policy *The Global 2000 Report to the
    President* (Penguin).
Detailed and comprehensive report to the President of the USA
    by the Council on Environmental Policy.

VI Life Style and Feelings

Jack Dominion, *Cycles of Affirmation*.
Asserts the value of self-affirmation from a biblical standpoint.

Richard Foster, *Celebration of Discipline* (Hodder & Stoughton).
Subtitled 'the path to spiritual growth' with a Foreword by
    David Watson.

Jane Madders, *Stress and Relaxation* (Martin Dunitz).

Anthony Storr, *Human Aggression* (Penguin).

Esther de Waal, *Seeking God. The Way of St Benedict*.
Profound, readable and contemporary.

VII Life Style and World Development

Third World First.
Beyond Brandt. An alternative strategy.

VIII Life Style and Health

Ivan Illich, *Limits to Medicine* (Penguin).
Provocative and persuasive.

Ian Kennedy, *The Unmasking of Medicine* (Granada).

Michael Wilson, *Health is for People* (Oxford).
(See also Debbie Taylor – *New Internationalist*, September 1983, pp. 7f.)

IX Life Style and the Proper Future of Work

Roger Clarke, *Work in Crisis*, (St Andrews Press).
Detailed critique of employment and unemployment from a Christian point of view. Extensive bibliography. Information also obtainable from Job Sharing Project, 77 Balfour St, London SE17.

NOTE   The literature of Liberation Theology is also relevant to the general theme of this book. A good but little-known development of the biblical basis is found in *It's a Long Road to Freedom*, by Bastiaan Wielenga, published by the Tamilnadu Theological Seminary, Arasaradi, Madurai 625 010, India.

RICH CHRISTIANS IN AN AGE OF HUNGER

Ronald Sider

Millions of people die of starvation each year. Even the most conservative statistics reflect a horrifying situation. One billion people have stunted bodies or damaged brains because of inadequate food. What should be the Christian response?

When this book was first published it caused turmoil in the Christian community across the world. In this revised and expanded edition, Ronald Sider provides updated information, and responds to many of his critics by reconsidering his arguments. His case for Christian action is stronger than ever.

'This book contains the most vital challenge which faces the church today. It is one of the most searching and disquieting books I have ever read . . . it calls, above all, for immediate and sacrificial action, if we know anything of God's love in our hearts.' – *From the foreword by David Watson*.

POOR MAN, RICH MAN

Peter Lee

With a foreword by Bishop Desmond Tutu

'Dorcas Selele is blind, black and old. She lives in Alexandra Township, a single square mile of residential chaos on the opposite corner of Johannesburg from the massive sprawl of Soweto . . . Life is not bad for Dorcas: sure, there are neither drains nor street lights in Alex, and in six months there were 165 murders, 118 reported rapes and 600 assaults. This past Christmas people bled to death in the passage at the clinic because the doctors couldn't sew any faster . . .'

With the particular problems of South Africa as his starting point, Peter Lee speaks directly to Christians in the affluent West and asks: is the gospel solely a spiritual programme, or have social and political issues a part to play? What is the mission and the purpose of the Church worldwide, and what means should be used to achieve it?